# NGINX High Performance

Optimize NGINX for high-performance, scalable web applications

**Rahul Sharma**

BIRMINGHAM - MUMBAI

# NGINX High Performance

First published: July 2015

Production reference: 1100715

Published by Packt Publishing Ltd.
Livery Place
35 Livery Street
Birmingham B3 2PB, UK.

ISBN 978-1-78528-183-9

www.packtpub.com

# Credits

**Author**

Rahul Sharma

**Reviewers**

Titouan Galopin

Tatsuhiko Kubo

**Commissioning Editor**

Veena Pagare

**Acquisition Editor**

Shaon Basu

**Content Development Editor**

Sumeet Sawant

**Technical Editor**

Shashank Desai

**Copy Editor**

Sarang Chari

**Project Coordinator**

Shweta H Birwatkar

**Proofreader**

Safis Editing

**Indexer**

Monica Ajmera Mehta

**Production Coordinator**

Nilesh R. Mohite

**Cover Work**

Nilesh R. Mohite

# About the Author

**Rahul Sharma** works as a principal consultant with Xebia India. He has 10 years of experience in building and designing applications on the Java and J2EE platforms. He is an open source enthusiast and has contributed to a variety of open source projects, such as Apache Crunch, Apache Provisionr, Apache HDT, and so on. In his career, he has worked with companies of various sizes, from enterprises to start-ups, and has used NGINX along the way. He often speaks at various technical meetups and shares his knowledge on his personal blog at `https://devlearnings.wordpress.com/`.

# About the Reviewers

**Titouan Galopin** is a certified PHP/Symfony French web architect from Paris. He has worked for various companies, including Ademis, Emakina, LIIP, and Coburo.

Titouan graduated in computer science and information technology from the Paris-Saclay University, and he is currently pursuing an engineering degree from the University of Technology of Compiègne.

First as a web developer and then as a web architect since 2012, Titouan has worked on NGINX intensively to improve its performance as much as possible. In the few years of his work, he has accumulated a lot of experience with NGINX, and he is now an expert in optimizing it to serve web content.

**Tatsuhiko Kubo** is a software engineer in infrastructure engineering and has a strong passion for open source software. His contribution to the development and publication of works on various kinds of open source software is his life's work. His usual work includes the development and operation of various kinds of middleware.

# www.PacktPub.com

## Support files, eBooks, discount offers, and more

For support files and downloads related to your book, please visit www.PacktPub.com.

Did you know that Packt offers eBook versions of every book published, with PDF and ePub files available? You can upgrade to the eBook version at www.PacktPub.com and as a print book customer, you are entitled to a discount on the eBook copy. Get in touch with us at service@packtpub.com for more details.

At www.PacktPub.com, you can also read a collection of free technical articles, sign up for a range of free newsletters and receive exclusive discounts and offers on Packt books and eBooks.

https://www2.packtpub.com/books/subscription/packtlib

Do you need instant solutions to your IT questions? PacktLib is Packt's online digital book library. Here, you can search, access, and read Packt's entire library of books.

## Why Subscribe?

- Fully searchable across every book published by Packt
- Copy and paste, print, and bookmark content
- On demand and accessible via a web browser

## Free Access for Packt account holders

If you have an account with Packt at www.PacktPub.com, you can use this to access PacktLib today and view 9 entirely free books. Simply use your login credentials for immediate access.

# Table of Contents

# Preface

NGINX is one of the most widely used web servers on the Internet. The server is often named when one is looking to deliver better performance with the same hardware. The server has a state-of-the-art event-based architecture, which enables it to deliver hundreds of thousands of concurrent connections on standard hardware.

As a first step, adopting NGINX leads to better results. However, as with any piece of software, NGINX can also be optimized to serve content faster. This book provides ways to optimize NGINX for last-mile performance. It also aims to provide insights into the NGINX architecture for you to understand it better. The book is not an NGINX learning book and is intended for people with some experience with NGINX. The book only explains those parts of the NGINX configuration that have an impact on performance.

Besides NGINX optimization, the book also talks about the process of benchmarking and about baselines to quantify the gains made. This is an end-to-end book that helps you to tweak the NGINX server's performance.

## What this book covers

*Chapter 1*, *Working with NGINX*, talks about NGINX's high-performance architecture. It also explains the various modules available in NGINX. The chapter lists details of the amenability of the server to customization. In the end, the chapter builds a simple configuration to deploy example web pages in NGINX.

*Chapter 2*, *Benchmarking the Server*, explains performance testing to generate baselines. Siege and JMeter are tools used to measure and benchmark the performance of your server. The chapter aims to generate metrics for the web pages deployed in *Chapter 1*, *Working with NGINX*, which can be compared to see performance changes.

*Chapter 3*, *Tweaking NGINX Configuration*, covers the parameters: Worker and Worker_process, the use method and multi_accept, Sendfile, directio and aio, tcp_nodely, and tcp_nopush.

*Chapter 4*, *Controlling Buffers, Timeouts, and Compression*, lists the features: keeplive, send timeouts, client buffers, gzip compression, and controlling logs.

*Chapter 5*, *Configuring the Network Stack*, lists details about tweaking the TCP options to achieve better network utilization. This chapter also talks about various server defaults that need to be customized.

*Chapter 6*, *Using NGINX Cache*, shows that NGINX can cache static content, as well as dynamic content. The server provides various directives to cache content. The chapter lists ways to use caches, namely FastCGI Cache, NGINX Proxy Cache, and Memcache, to render content.

*Chapter 7*, *Extending NGINX*, provides details of HttpLuaModule, which can be used to extend NGINX for all kinds of activities. The module enables support for Lua, which is a powerful, fast, lightweight, embeddable scripting language. The chapter aims to build an SEO check using Lua.

# What you need for this book

You'll require the following software:

- NGINX 1.7.x
- JMeter
- Siege
- PHP and PHP-FPM
- Python and Flask
- Memcache

# Who this book is for

A system administrator or developer looking for ways to extract the maximum performance from NGINX will find this book useful. If you are facing various challenges, such as handling more users from the same system and aiming to load your website pages faster, then this book is for you.

# Conventions

In this book, you will find a number of styles of text that distinguish between different kinds of information. Here are some examples of these styles, and an explanation of their meaning.

Code words in text, database table names, folder names, filenames, file extensions, pathnames, dummy URLs, user input, and Twitter handles are shown as follows: "The worker then uses the available event-notification interfaces, such as epoll and kqueue, to process each connection in an efficient event loop."

A block of code is set as follows:

```
location /hello {
        alias "$ABSOLUTE_PATH_TO_CODE";
}
```

Any command-line input or output is written as follows:

```
curl -I http://nginx.org
```

**New terms** and **important words** are shown in bold. Words that you see on the screen, in menus or dialog boxes for example, appear in the text like this: "This module allows us to return either the **444 error** or the **204 error** in low-memory conditions."

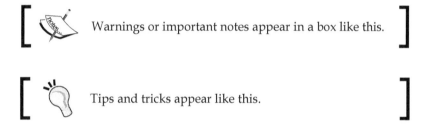

Warnings or important notes appear in a box like this.

Tips and tricks appear like this.

# Reader feedback

Feedback from our readers is always welcome. Let us know what you think about this book—what you liked or may have disliked. Reader feedback is important for us to develop titles that you really get the most out of.

To send us general feedback, simply send an e-mail to feedback@packtpub.com, and mention the book title via the subject of your message.

If there is a topic that you have expertise in and you are interested in either writing or contributing to a book, see our author guide on www.packtpub.com/authors.

# Customer support

Now that you are the proud owner of a Packt book, we have a number of things to help you to get the most from your purchase.

# Downloading the example code

You can download the example code files for all Packt books you have purchased from your account at http://www.packtpub.com. If you purchased this book elsewhere, you can visit http://www.packtpub.com/support and register to have the files e-mailed directly to you.

# Errata

Although we have taken every care to ensure the accuracy of our content, mistakes do happen. If you find a mistake in one of our books—maybe a mistake in the text or the code—we would be grateful if you could report this to us. By doing so, you can save other readers from frustration and help us improve subsequent versions of this book. If you find any errata, please report them by visiting http://www.packtpub.com/submit-errata, selecting your book, clicking on the **Errata Submission Form** link, and entering the details of your errata. Once your errata are verified, your submission will be accepted and the errata will be uploaded to our website or added to any list of existing errata under the Errata section of that title.

To view the previously submitted errata, go to https://www.packtpub.com/books/content/support and enter the name of the book in the search field. The required information will appear under the **Errata** section.

# Piracy

Piracy of copyright material on the Internet is an ongoing problem across all media. At Packt, we take the protection of our copyright and licenses very seriously. If you come across any illegal copies of our works, in any form, on the Internet, please provide us with the location address or website name immediately so that we can pursue a remedy.

Please contact us at copyright@packtpub.com with a link to the suspected pirated material.

We appreciate your help in protecting our authors, and our ability to bring you valuable content.

# Questions

You can contact us at questions@packtpub.com if you are having a problem with any aspect of the book, and we will do our best to address it.

# 1
# Working with NGINX

Igor Sysoev started developing NGINX in 2002. The first version was aimed at delivering static content on web scale. It was released to the public in 2004, thus solving Daniel Kegel's C10K problem of 10,000 simultaneous connections. NGINX adapted a modular, asynchronous, event-based, nonblocking architecture, which works well to deliver tens of thousands of concurrent connections on a server with typical hardware.

In this chapter, we will cover the following topics:

- The NGINX architecture
- Installing NGINX from source
- Configuring NGINX for HTTP
- Deploying a "Hello world!" page

# The NGINX architecture

NGINX has its foundation in event-based architecture (EBA). In EBA, components interact predominantly using event notifications instead of direct method calls. These event notifications, occurring from different tasks, are then queued for processing by an event handler. The event handler runs in an event loop, where it processes an event, de-queues it, and then moves on to the next event. Thus, the work executed by a thread is very similar to that of a scheduler, multiplexing multiple connections to a single flow of execution. The following diagram shows this:

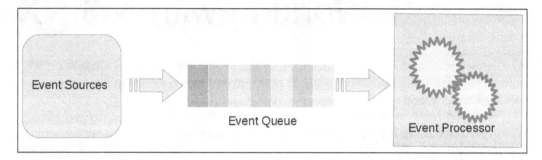

When compared with the thread-based architecture, EBA gives better performance output. In EBA, there are a fixed number of threads performing tasks and no new threads are formed. Thus, we achieve better utilization of the CPU and an improved memory footprint. There is also no overhead of excessive context switching and no need for a thread stack for each connection. Ideally, the CPU becomes the only apparent bottleneck of an event-driven application.

NGINX runs one master process and several worker processes. The master process reads/evaluates the configuration and maintains the worker processes. All request processing is done by the worker processes. NGINX does not start workers for every request. Instead, it has a fixed pool of workers for request processing. Each worker accepts new requests from a shared listen queue. The worker then uses the available event-notification interfaces, such as `epoll` and `kqueue`, to process each connection in an efficient event loop. The idea is to optimize the utilization of the server's resources using nonblocking/asynchronous mechanisms when possible. By doing so, each worker is able to process thousands of connections. The following diagram shows this:

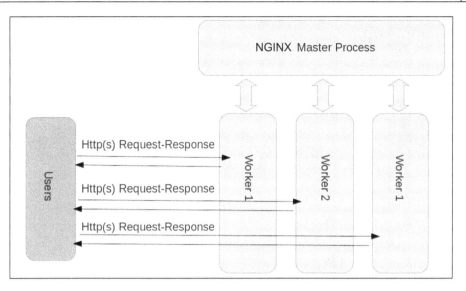

NGINX has an extensible modular architecture. There is a core module (ngx_core_
module), which is responsible for connection handling. Then, there are modules
for every kind of processing that NGINX offers, for instance an HTTP module
(ngx_http_core_module) for HTTP processing, an e-mail module (ngx_mail_core_
module) for e-mail processing, a proxy module (ngx_http_proxy_module), and
so on. The modular system is quite extensible and allows third-party developers
to extend NGINX beyond its existing capabilities. Each worker loads a chain of
modules as specified in the NGINX configuration. Every request that a worker
handles goes through the loaded chain of modules.

# Installing NGINX from source

NGINX can be downloaded from http://nginx.org/. The site provides a stable
package and a mainline version package. Both versions are quite stable, and either
of them can be used to build NGINX for production environments. The mainline
version contains all active development. This essentially means that all new features
and noncritical bug fixes are developed here. At times, this may also cause certain
third-party modules to break due to a change in the internal APIs. The stable version
only gets the critical bug fixes. New features and noncritical bug fixes are not ported
to the stable version. NGINX has a well-maintained documentation available at
http://nginx.org/en/docs/. The documentation is a great source of information
related to NGINX features, internals, and recipes.

**Nginx.org** runs the released mainline version. You can check this using the following `curl` command:

```
curl -I http://nginx.org
```

The preceding command will print HTTP headers, which list the server they run on:

```
HTTP/1.1 200 OK
Server: nginx/1.7.7
Content-Type: text/html; charset=utf-8
```

# Build requirements

Before we start building NGINX, we need to make sure that your system meets the requirements mentioned in the following pages.

## The ANSI C compiler and build system

As NGINX is written in C, GNU C Compiler (GCC) is recommended to build this. So, make sure you have `gcc` installed on your box. In addition to this, make sure that PATH contains essential build tools, such as `make`.

Install the build-essential package using the following code to get the complete set of tools:

```
$ sudo apt-get install build-essential
```

NGNIX provides options to customize/optimize the compilation and linking done by the C compiler. You could also specify a C compiler and preprocessor that is not in PATH:

- `--with-cc`: This specifies an alternative C compiler location to the one in PATH.

- `--with-cpp`: This provides the C preprocessor's location.

- `--with-cc-opt`: This specifies the additional options that are passed to the C compiler. You can pass options to include libraries, for example, `-I /usr/local/include`.

- `--with-ld-opt`: This specifies additional options that are passed to Linker. You can pass options to link libraries, for example, `-L /usr/local/lib`.

- `--with-cpu-opt`: This platform argument can be specified so that a build can be optimized for a specific architecture.

## libatomic_ops and AIO – optional requirements

NGINX can use `libatomic_ops` for memory update operations. The library allows atomic updates, thus removing the lock handling involved in accessing shared memory. You can install the required package and use it with the `--with-libatomic` configuration parameter. Optionally, you can also download the library from `https://github.com/ivmai/libatomic_ops` and point to it using the `--with-libatomic` configuration parameter.

Linux offers asynchronous I/O (AIO). This allows applications to overlap I/O operations with other processing, thus enabling better utilization of resources. NGINX can use this by using the `--with-file-aio` configuration parameter.

Install the `libaio1`, `libatomic-ops`, and `libatomic-ops-dev` packages to get the required libraries, as shown in the following code:

```
$ sudo apt-get install libaio1 libatomic-ops libatomic-
ops-dev
```

## Perl – an optional requirement

NGINX-embedded Perl (`ngx_http_perl_module`) requires Perl to be installed on your box. The module can be used to build Perl-based configurations in NGINX configuration files. You could also download/build the Perl binary from `http://www.perl.org/` and point to it using the `--with-perl` parameter. Perl modules, used in configurations, can be located with `--with-perl` modules configuration parameters.

Install the Perl package as follows to get the required binaries:

```
$ sudo apt-get install perl
```

To know about the available modules, use the following code:

```
$ apt-cache search geo::ipfree
```

## The Perl Compatible Regular Expressions library – an optional requirement

The NGINX HTTP rewrite (`ngx_http_rewite_module`) module requires the support of the **Perl Compatible Regular Expressions** (PCRE) library. You could install the package, or you could download the sources from `http://www.pcre.org/` and point to it using the `--with-pcre` configuration parameter. Additional parameters can be passed with the `--with-pcre-opt` argument; they are passed to the PCRE library.

Install the `libpcre3` and `libpcre3-dev` packages as follows to get the required libraries:

```
$ sudo apt-get install libpcre3 libpcre3-dev
```

## OpenSSL – an optional requirement

NGINX provides strong cryptography using SSL and TLS protocols. This requires the OpenSSL package to be available on your box. Optionally, you could download the OpenSSL source from `http://www.openssl.org/` and point to it using the `--with-openssl` option. Additional parameters can be passed with the `--with-openssl-opt` argument; they are passed to the OpenSSL library.

 Install the `openssl` and `libssl-dev` packages as follows to get the required libs:

```
$ sudo apt-get install openssl libssl-dev
```

NGINX, by default, does not enable the SSL module. It can be enabled using the `--with-http_ssl_module` configuration.

## Zlib – an optional requirement

NGINX can compress HTTP responses in `gzip`. In order to do this, it requires the support of the Zlib library. You could either install the package or download the sources from `http://www.zlib.net/` and point to it using the `--with-zlib` configuration parameter.

 Install the `zlib1g` and `zlib1g-dev` packages as follows to get the required libs:

```
$ sudo apt-get install zlib1g zlib1g-dev
```

# Configuring NGINX

Download and extract the NGINX `src` package `.tar.gz` archive from `http://nginx.org/en/download.html`. Use the following command:

```
$ wget http://nginx.org/download/nginx-1.7.9.tar.gz
```

Next, configure NGINX in the following manner:

```
$ cd nginx-1.7.9
$ ./configure
```

The `configure` command will generate a default NGINX configuration in the form of Makefile. The following output shows the generated configuration of the NGINX binary:

```
Configuration summary
+ using PCRE library: ../pcre-8.35
+ OpenSSL library is not used
+ md5: using system crypto library
+ sha1: using system crypto library
+ using system zlib library


nginx path prefix: "/usr/local/nginx"
nginx binary file: "/usr/local/nginx/sbin/nginx"
nginx configuration prefix: "/usr/local/nginx/conf"
nginx configuration file: "/usr/local/nginx/conf/nginx.conf"
nginx pid file: "/usr/local/nginx/logs/nginx.pid"
nginx error log file: "/usr/local/nginx/logs/error.log"
nginx http access log file: "/usr/local/nginx/logs/access.log"
nginx http client request body temporary files: "client_body_temp"
nginx http proxy temporary files: "proxy_temp"
nginx http fastcgi temporary files: "fastcgi_temp"
nginx http uwsgi temporary files: "uwsgi_temp"
nginx http scgi temporary files: "scgi_temp"
```

The configuration step provides loads of options to alter default paths and enable/disable all kinds of modules available with NGINX. Using these, you can configure NGINX as per your requirements. This step requires some thought as, once NGINX binaries are built for a configuration, they cannot be altered for default paths or for the support of disabled modules.

## Configuring NGINX defaults

NGINX provides options to change default paths, configuration filenames, log files, and so on. It is not mandatory to provide these options. They have a default value, which is used if the option is not specified:

- `--prefix` : `/usr/local/nginx`: This specifies the path where NGINX will be installed. All other paths are relative to this location.

- `--sbin-path` : `prefix/sbin/nginx`: This specifies the name of the NGINX executable binary file.

- `--conf-path` : `prefix/conf/nginx.conf`: NGINX can run a configuration file using the `-c` filename runtime arguments. If that is not specified, NGINX tries to load a default configuration specified by this option.

- `--pid-path` : `prefix/logs/nginx.pid`: The NGINX runtime configuration can specify a PID file, the location to store the process ID of the main process. If the `pid` directive is missing from the configuration file, NGINX stores the information at the location specified by this option.

- `--lock-path` : `prefix/logs/nginx.lock`: NGINX maintains a lock for shared access to resources. The runtime configuration can specify the lock file. If the `lock` directive is missing from the configuration file, NGINX stores the information at the location specified by this option.

- `--error-log-path` : `prefix/logs/error.log`: An error log path can be specified in the NGINX runtime configuration. If the `error_log` directive is missing in the specified configuration, then NGINX writes the log at the location specified by this option.

- `--http-log-path` : `prefix/logs/access.log`: The `HTTP-access` log paths can be specified in the NGINX runtime configuration. If the `access_log` directive is missing in the specified configuration, NGINX writes logs at the location specified by this option.

- `--with-debug`: This option enables a detailed debug log in NGINX. This option is not enabled by default.

- `--user` : `nobody`: The NGINX runtime configuration can specify an unprivileged user run NGINX worker processes.

- `--group` : `nobody`: The NGINX runtime configuration can specify a group that will own NGINX worker processes.

- `--build`: This option assigns a name to the generated binary. The name would be available in the NGINX `-v` command.

## Configuring NGINX modules

NGINX has an extensive set of features. It can be used as a web server, a web cache, a load balancer, an e-mail proxy, and so on. All these features of NGINX are compiled and configured as modules. Certain modules are enabled by default, while some need to be enabled. Modules should be carefully selected when building a high-performance system to keep a low memory footprint.

# Configuring NGINX for the Web

NGINX, by default, installs the HTTP module. The HTTP server can be disabled using the `--without-http` configuration parameter. Along with the HTTP module, NGINX also enables the following modules by default. The modules can be disabled selectively using the specified configuration parameter. Here is a list of a few parameters:

- `--without-http_access_module`: This module allows us to control access from a limited set of IP addresses.

- `--without-http_autoindex_module`: This module builds the index file, which can generate a directory listing for requests ending with a forward slash (/).

- `--without-http_auth_basic_module`: This module allows access control using the basic authentication protocol.

- `--without-http_browser_module`: This module enables us to create variables based on the value of the **User-Agent** request header field.

- `--without-http_charset_module`: This module enables the conversion of the response data between different character encodings and the setting of the **Content-Type** response header field.

- `--without-http_empty_gif_module`: This module allows NGINX to serve a 1 x 1 transparent GIF from memory.

- `--without-http_fastcgi_module`: This module allows NGINX to send requests to the FastCGI server.

- `--without-http_geo_module`: This module allows us to set up configuration variables based on the client IP address. The variables can then be used in other modules for certain actions.

- `--without-http_gzip_module`: This module allows us to compress responses in the `gzip` format, thus reducing the amount of bytes transferred.

- `--without-http-cache`: NGINX is capable of using the HTTP cache, that is, setting the correct request headers to enable content caching. This can be used when NGINX is set up as a proxy to an upstream content provider. The option can disable the cache, but it is not advisable as the cache is quite handy in most setups.

- `--without-http_limit_conn_module`: This module allows us to control the number of concurrent connections from a single IP. Post limits, it sends the **503 error** response.

- `--without-http_limit_req_module`: This module allows us to define the request processing rate for particular keys. It keeps track of requests from a single IP, queuing them if the request rate exceeds the defined processing rate. After the maximum queue size has been reached, it sends a **503 error** response.

- `--without-http_map_module`: This module allows us to set up configuration variables that derive value from other existing variables.

- `--without-http_memcached_module`: This module allows NGINX to serve requests directly from a memcached server. The memcached server should contain the response in advance by means external to NGINX.

- `--without-http_proxy_module`: This module enables NGINX to send requests to other servers.

- `--without-http_referer_module`: This module allows NGINX to filter requests based on the values in the **Referrer** header field.

- `--without-http_rewrite_module`: This module allows NGINX to manipulate URLs, using regular expressions, based on certain conditions.

- `--without-http_scgi_module`: This module allows NGINX to send requests to the SCGI server.

- `--without-http_split_clients_module`: This module allows NGINX to configure variables for A/B testing.

- `--without-http_ssi_module`: This module enables NGINX to process SSI commands

- `--without-http_upstream_ip_hash_module --without-http_upstream_keepalive_module --without-http_upstream_least_conn_module`

These modules enable load-balancing capabilities in NGINX. A number of servers can be grouped together to provide upstream content to NGINX. The upstream group can distribute requests between them using any of the following methods:

  - client IP address hash
  - keep-alive parameters
  - number of connected clients

NGINX has separate modules depending on the method selected for request distribution.

- `--without-http_userid_module`

  This module allows NGINX to use cookies for client identification.

- `--without-http_uwsgi_module`

  This module allows NGINX to send requests to the uWSGI server.

  Besides the preceding modules, which are enabled by default, the NGINX catalog has modules that can offer a range of features, such as SSL support, streaming media, and so on. These modules are disabled by default and need to be enabled at compile time. The following is the list of modules that can be enabled at compile time.

- `--with-http_addition_module`: This module can modify the response returned for a given request. It adds a response from another subrequest before and after the actual response.

- `--with-http_auth_request_module`: The module can enable client authorization based on the subrequest. The client accesses protected resources, which trigger a subrequest for authorization. Depending on the response code received, access is allowed (2xx) or denied (**401 error/403 error**).

- `--with-http_degradation_module`: This module allows us to return either the **444 error** or the **204 error** in low-memory conditions. This module is not available on Linux platforms.

- `--with-http_perl_module`: This module allows you to insert Perl code into your NGINX configuration files and to make Perl calls from SSI.

- `--with-http_flv_module`: This module provides support to stream Flash media files.

- `--with-http_geoip_module`: This module allows us to use Maxmind GeoIP-Databases to build custom variables based on client IP addresses.

 Note that in order to use this module, you need to have the Maxmind library in your path.

- `--with-http_google_perftools_module`: This module allows you to use Google's performance tools (`http://code.google.com/p/gperftools/`) to profile NGINX workers.

- `--with-http_gzip_static_module`: This module enables NGINX to serve precompressed static content in the `.gz` form.
- `--with-http_image_filter_module`: This module allows image transformation using the `libgd` library.

>  Note that in order to use this module, you need to have the `libgd` library in your PATH.

- `--with-http_mp4_module`: This module enables the streaming of MP4 files.
- `--with-http_random_index_module`: This module enables NGINX to randomly select and serve any file in a directory as the index file.
- `--with-http_realip_module`: This module can be used to correctly determine the client IP. If NGINX is used behind a proxy or a load balancer, then the module can extract the client IP from the correct header field.
- `--with-http_secure_link_module`: This module is used to access control of locations by generating checksums.
- `--with-http_spdy_module`: This module enables support for the SPDY protocol.
- `--with-http_ssl_module`: This module enables HTTPS support in NGINX.
- `--with-http_stub_status_module`: This module builds basic server statistics.
- `--with-http_sub_module`: This module modifies the generated response by replacing certain search strings with replacement strings.
- `--with-http_dav_module`: This module extends support for the WebDAV protocol over HTTP.
- `--with-http_xslt_module`: This module modifies the generated response using XSLT transformations.

>  Note that you need to have the `libxml2` and `libxslt` libraries in your PATH.

# Configuring NGINX for e-mail

NGINX has the capability to serve as an e-mail proxy. It supports POP3, IMAP, and SMTP protocols along with SSL capabilities. The e-mail modules are disabled by default. They need to be configured with the following parameters:

- `--with-mail`: This module enables e-mail capabilities. It enables POP3, IMAP, and SMTP modules.

- `--with-mail_ssl_module`: This module enables the support for the SSL/TLS protocols for e-mail services.

- `--without-mail_pop3_module`: This module enables the support for the POP3 protocol. The module is enabled by the e-mail module.

- `--without-mail_imap_module`: This module enables the support for the IMAP protocol. This module is enabled by the e-mail module.

- `--without-mail_smtp_module`: This module enables the support for the SMTP protocol. The module is enabled by the e-mail module.

# Configuring third-party modules

NGINX is completely modular in nature, which essentially means that you can build your own modules to extend its existing capabilities. The NGINX community has built a large number of third-party modules that can perform various tasks. If you want to use a few of these modules, you need to compile them with the NGINX source. Download the module source and point to the source using the `--add-module` configure parameter. You can add as many modules as you want.

> The NGINX official release does not support these modules, so make sure that you test the binaries before setting them up for production. If you are building from the mainline source, then modules relying on internal APIs can break while moving from one version to another.

# NGINX – the complete package

Now that you know how to configure the available modules in NGINX, you may want to customize the binary as per your needs. While you are enabling/disabling modules, do make a note of all the libraries that NGINX will rely on. For the modules available from the NGINX catalog, it may be a good idea to download the required sources and point to them using correct parameters. The following command configures an NGINX binary:

```
$ ./configure \
    --prefix=/etc/nginx \
```

```
    --user=www-data \
    --group=www-data \
    --without-http_uwsgi_module \
    --without-http_scgi_module \
    --without-http_fastcgi_module \
    --without-http_geo_module \
    --without-http_browser_module \
    --without-http_upstream_keepalive_module \
    --without-http_browser_module \
    --without-http_ssi_module \
    --with-openssl=../openssl-1.0.2a \
    --with-pcre=../pcre-8.36 \
    --with-http_ssl_module \
    --with-http_realip_module \
    --with-http_sub_module \
    --with-http_gzip_static_module \
    --with-http_secure_link_module \
    --with-http_stub_status_module \
    --with-libatomic=../libatomic_ops-7.2 \
    --with-file-aio
```

The following output summary lists the libraries used and the NGINX defaults generated. Makefile, which is generated as a result of the preceding code, can be used to build and install the NGINX binary. Here's the output summary of the preceding command:

```
Configuration summary
  + using PCRE library: ../pcre-8.36
  + using OpenSSL library: ../openssl-1.0.2a
  + md5: using OpenSSL library
  + sha1: using OpenSSL library
  + using system zlib library
  + using libatomic_ops library: ../libatomic_ops-7.2

nginx path prefix: "/etc/nginx"
nginx binary file: "/etc/nginx/sbin/nginx"
nginx configuration prefix: "/etc/nginx/conf"
nginx configuration file: "/etc/nginx/conf/nginx.conf"
nginx pid file: "/etc/nginx/logs/nginx.pid"
nginx error log file: "/etc/nginx/logs/error.log"
nginx http access log file: "/etc/nginx/logs/access.log"
nginx http client request body temporary files: "client_body_temp"
nginx http proxy temporary files: "proxy_temp"
```

# Building and installing NGINX

The `configure` command generated Makefile for the specified configuration. Makefile can now be used to install NGINX in the following manner:

```
$ make
$ sudo make install
```

The preceding command shows the output listing the locations of installation:

```
test -d '/etc/nginx' || mkdir -p '/etc/nginx'
test -d '/etc/nginx/sbin'          || mkdir -p '/etc/nginx/sbin'
test ! -f '/etc/nginx/sbin/nginx'      || mv
'/etc/nginx/sbin/nginx'        '/etc/nginx/sbin/nginx.old'
cp objs/nginx '/etc/nginx/sbin/nginx'
test -d '/etc/nginx/conf'          || mkdir -p '/etc/nginx/conf'
cp conf/koi-win '/etc/nginx/conf'
cp conf/koi-utf '/etc/nginx/conf'
cp conf/win-utf '/etc/nginx/conf'
test -f '/etc/nginx/conf/mime.types'        || cp
conf/mime.types '/etc/nginx/conf'
cp conf/mime.types '/etc/nginx/conf/mime.types.default'
test -f '/etc/nginx/conf/fastcgi_params'      || cp
conf/fastcgi_params '/etc/nginx/conf'
cp conf/fastcgi_params     '/etc/nginx/conf/fastcgi_params.default'
test -f '/etc/nginx/conf/fastcgi.conf'         || cp
conf/fastcgi.conf '/etc/nginx/conf'
```

> The `make` command prints lot of debugging information, for example, the library paths, the default configuration paths, and so on. You can run it with the `-s` option to disable all the information.

After installation, NGINX is available in the specified prefix directory. You can go to the specified location and run it with the `sudo` command. Alternatively, you can add it to PATH using `update-alternatives` and then run it. The following command shows this:

```
$ sudo update-alternatives --install /usr/bin/nginx nginx
/etc/nginx/sbin/nginx 1
$ sudo nginx
```

You can check this by loading `http://localhost` in your browser. It should display the following NGINX page:

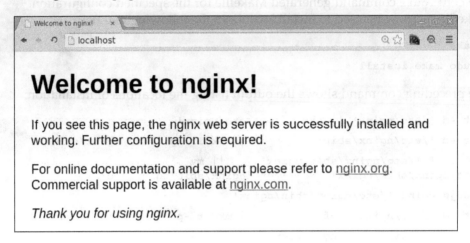

# Deploying in NGINX

Now that we have successfully installed NGINX, we want to try out some deployments in NGINX.

In this section, we have a Hello world! web page that we will deploy in NGINX. The code uses the Bootstrap library, which needs to be packaged with the code. The complete package has the following structure:

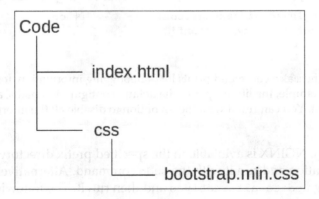

The following is the HTML markup of `index.html`:

```
<!DOCTYPE html>
<html lang="en">
 <head>
  <title>Using Nginx</title>
  <link href="css/bootstrap.min.css" rel="stylesheet">
 </head>
 <body>
  <div class="container">
   <div class="jumbotron">
   <h1>Hello world!</h1>
   <p>Deploying in Nginx<p>
   </div>
  </div>
 </body>
</html>
```

In this HTML markup, we will display the heading "Hello, world!" and a bit of text on the web page, which has the title *Using Nginx*. The Bootstrap CSS has been used to style the content. You can download it from `http://getbootstrap.com/getting-started/` or use the `wget` command from a CDN and add it to the `css` folder:

```
$ wget https://maxcdn.bootstrapcdn.com/bootstrap/3.3.2/css/bootstrap.min.
css
```

Details of the HTML source code will not be covered here as they are beyond the scope of the book. The purpose of this code is to deploy a simple web page in NGINX.

# Deploying NGINX

We want to load the page created previously at the location `http://localhost/hello`. In order to do so, we need to write a configuration block using the following directives:

- `location`: This defines a configuration for a URI. The location URI can be a prefix or a regular expression.

- `alias`: This defines the directory path for the specified location directive. This is the location from where all the files are served.

- `include`: This allows the inclusion of the configuration blocks defined in one file in another file.

NGINX, by default, loads the deployment from `nginx.conf` in the installation directory.

> In the preceding section, NGINX was installed in `/etc/nginx`, thus `nginx.conf` should be available in `/etc/nginx/conf/nginx.conf`.
>
> NGINX allows us to write configurations across multiple files as logical units. We can include these files in a main file to define the complete configuration. Rather than writing configuration blocks in `nginx.conf`, we will create new files and then include them in the required locations in `nginx.conf`.

For our purposes, we will create `nginx-localhost-server.conf` in the `/etc/nginx/conf` directory with the following configuration block:

```
location /hello {
    alias "$ABSOLUTE_PATH_TO_CODE";
}
```

Here, we have defined the `/hello` location and set it to serve from `index.html` at `$ABSOLUTE_PATH_TO_CODE`. When the page is loaded, it tries to load the CSS from `/hello/css/bootstrap.min.css`. The location directive successfully matches the `/hello` prefix and serves the CSS from the `$ABSOLUTE_PATH_TO_CODE/css` path.

The `/hello` prefix needs to available in the localhost server's name; thus, we need to include `nginx-localhost-server.conf` in the block, which defines the localhost server in `nginx.conf`. The following code shows this:

```
server_name localhost;

# include the hello location
include nginx-localhost-server.conf;

location / {
    root   html;
    index index.html index.htm;
}
```

Now, all that is left for us to do is reload NGINX. It is always a good idea to test the NGINX configuration before loading. Testing can flag up possible errors arising from invalid configurations, which would be discovered while loading NGINX. Use the `-t` switch to test the configuration, as shown in the following code:

```
$ sudo nginx -t
```

If the test is successful, the command will print the following output; otherwise, it will print the errors found, if any:

```
nginx: the configuration file /etc/nginx/conf/nginx.conf syntax is ok
nginx: configuration file /etc/nginx/conf/nginx.conf test is
successful
```

Once we have verified the configuration, reload NGINX with the following configuration:

```
$ sudo nginx -s reload
```

Verify the page at `http://localhost/hello`. It should show the following content:

> **Downloading the example code**
>
> You can download the example code files for all Packt books you have purchased from your account at `http://www.packtpub.com`. If you purchased this book elsewhere, you can visit `http://www.packtpub.com/support` and register to have the files e-mailed directly to you.

# Summary

This chapter gave insights into the components of the performance-oriented NGINX architecture and the EBA model. NGINX was compiled from source with components that suit our requirements. The custom build package was installed and a sample web page was deployed to it.

The purpose of this chapter was to give you a crash course in NGINX. In the subsequent chapters, we will see ways to measure your NGINX website's performance and optimize it for the last mile.

# Benchmarking the Server

2

Benchmarking the server is the process of generating metrics of the throughput, responsiveness, and reliability of the application response. This is the precursor to server optimization since the generated metrics serve as a baseline that can be used to know the effectiveness of any optimization done.

The following sections list the ways and tools to benchmark your server:

- Performance testing and baselines
- Generating metrics using Siege
- Generating metrics using Apache JMeter

## Performance testing

The idea of performance testing is to put the system under pressure and determine various quality attributes, such as stability, responsiveness, and so on. These attributes can serve multiple purposes, such as the following:

- Validating whether the application meets a criterion
- Validating whether the system can perform in extreme conditions
- Comparing different applications
- Determining application bottlenecks
- Performance tuning

Thus, performance testing can serve a number of goals. Before we start testing, we need to ascertain the performance goals we want to achieve. Depending on our purpose, our tools and methodologies will change.

Performance testing has the following variations:

- **Load testing**: This is the simplest form of testing, where the system is put under a specified load. The idea is to know whether the system will perform well under anticipated workloads. The aim of load testing is to know the largest user load that the site can handle with accepted performance metrics.

- **Stress testing**: In this form of testing, the system is subjected to an extensive load to determine its upper limits. The idea is to find out the robustness and responsiveness under conditions beyond those anticipated during normal operations. This is a negative form of testing, where the intention is to find out at what loads the system will break.

In order to benchmark our server, we will subject it to a kind of load testing known as performance testing. The goal here is not to expose any defects but to establish the following parameters:

- **Throughput**: This is defined as the rate at which the server can serve content, that is, concurrent requests per second that a server can handle. This usually defines the upper limits of the web server.

- **Error rate**: This is defined as the ratio of nonsuccessful requests to the total number of requests. The error may have occurred due to server unavailability because of high load or due to network timeouts. The metric is used in conjunction with the throughput as it is required to have the minimum error rate with a higher throughput.

- **Response time**: This is defined as the time interval from the time instance when a request initiates to the time instance when the first part of the response is received, subtracting out latency, if any. A request is generally queued, and then it is serviced. Thus, the response time defines the time interval that a request spends in the queue and the time that the server takes to generate a response for that request.

# Using timeouts

When the server is under load, the average response time increases as the server is busy responding to the large number of requests it has received. When the server has optimizations, the test can be run again, and you can compare whether the average response time has improved or not. But, how can you go about comparing the error rate and the throughput? The two results may not show you any error rate or a small change in the throughput. This is because the server responds to all requests — just that it takes more time in certain instances.

In order to compare the error rate and the throughput, we need to take care of the response time. This can be done using the timeouts defined in HTTP. The HTTP protocol defines the following two timeouts:

- **Connection timeout**: This is the time it takes to create a connection (socket) to the web server
- **Response timeout**: This is the time it takes for the server to send back a response

For any request, if a timeout occurs, it is treated as a failure. Thus, while determining the error rate and the throughput in different tests, the timeouts should remain the same. Basically, when we run the test to determine a metric, the other factors should remain the same; otherwise, the numbers are difficult to compare.

# Baselines

A baseline is defined as the accepted attributes that describe a system at a particular point in time. Thus, the baseline serves as a point of reference. The idea is to capture performance metrics after every change and determine their effectiveness by comparing them to the baseline. Changes can only be compared one at a time. While working with baselines, we need to make sure that all aspects except for the single change must remain the same. Thus, the new metrics data, after the change, when compared to the baseline data, will show whether the performance improves or declines.

Our goal at the end of the chapter is to generate baselines that can be used to find out the efficacy of optimizations.

 Always run performance tests on a machine other than the server under test. If you run them on the same machine, the numbers generated will be misleading.

# A note about tools

Performance tests executed on various tools cannot be compared directly with each other. The tools vary significantly in how they simulate load and how metrics are determined; thus, the results vary largely when compared with each other. But the trend generated by tests on one tool is comparable to a trend from another tool. If a tool demonstrates a decrease in performance, then the other tool should provide a similar result.

Load simulation opens sockets on the client side. The sockets, in turn, are treated as file descriptors. Thus, make sure there are enough file descriptors available on the box. The limit can be enhanced by the `ulimit -n` command or by changing the `security.limits` file.

# Generating metrics using Siege

There are many tools for load testing your application. Some of these are free, open source solutions, while a few have commercial licenses. **Siege** is an open source utility, which can be used to stress test a server. It has been created by Jeff Fulmer and can be downloaded from `http://www.joedog.org/siege-home`.

Given a URL or a set of URLs, Siege can simulate the provided number of users to load test these locations. The utility generates metrics for the elapsed time, the total data transferred, the server response time, its transaction rate, its throughput, and its concurrency. Basically, the tool is aimed at generating server behavior when there is a traffic spike.

# Installing Siege

The latest version of Siege can be downloaded from `http://download.joedog.org/siege/siege-latest.tar.gz`. The `.tar.gz` can then be extracted to build and install the latest version of the utility. At the time of writing the book, version 3.0.9 is the latest one:

```
$ wget http://download.joedog.org/siege/siege-latest.tar.gz
$ tar -xvf siege-latest.tar.gz
$ cd siege-3.0.9/
$ ./configure
```

The `./configure` command generates a configuration for Siege. The process checks for all required libraries. The command provides loads of options; use the `-h` flag to list them. There are a few useful parameters that can be used to customize Siege. They are as follows:

- `prefix`: This installs Siege to the specified path and configures the default configuration files. If not specified, Siege is installed at `/usr/local`.
- `bindir`: This installs the binary in the specified directory.
- `mandir`: This installs the man pages in the specified directory.

- `with-ssl`: This lets Siege run for the HTTP protocol by default. If you want to use it for HTTPS, then OpenSSL is required. Siege tries to pick OpenSSL if it is available on the system; otherwise, one can be specified using this option.

- `without-ssl`: This specifies that SSL support is not to be built in Siege.

Post the `./configure` command, the tool can be installed by the following commands:

```
$ make
$ sudo make install
```

The `make` command generates the binary for the specified configuration, and `make install` installs it to the system path. The process lists down the location where the installation has happened.

Post installation, Siege may not be available on your path if it is installed to an alternative location, such as `/etc/siege`. In order to add it to the path, use the `update-alternatives` command, as shown here:

```
$ sudo update-alternatives --install /usr/bin/siege siege
/etc/siege/bin/siege1
```

Check Siege by running the following command:

```
$ siege -V
```

It should print the version as shown in the following output:

```
SIEGE 3.0.9

Copyright (C) 2014 by Jeffrey Fulmer, et al.
This is free software; see the source for copying conditions.
There is NO warranty; not even for MERCHANTABILITY or FITNESS
FOR A PARTICULAR PURPOSE.
```

> Siege is also available in Ubuntu repositories, but the package is a rather old one, for example, Ubuntu Precise offers Siege 2.7. This can be installed using the `apt-get` command as follows:
> ```
> $ sudo apt-get install siege
> ```

# Running Siege

The `siege` command can be executed on the terminal. The command lists all kinds of parameters that are available. You could run the command on the page deployed in the previous chapter, as follows:

```
$ siege http://192.168.2.100/hello/
```

By default, Siege keeps running for quite a while and prints a lot of logging information. You will be required to press *Ctrl + C* to close the program. The program executes the default load and prints the performance results, as shown in the following code:

```
Transactions:               4443 hits
Availability:               100.00 %
Elapsed time:               149.94 secs
Data transferred:           15.56 MB
Response time:              0.00 secs
Transaction rate:           29.63 trans/sec
Throughput:                 0.10 MB/sec
Concurrency:                0.05
Successful transactions:    4443
Failed transactions         0
Longest transaction:        0.01
Shortest transaction:       0.00
```

In the preceding command, Siege executed the default configuration. Use the -C or --config options to find out your default configuration:

```
$ siege -C
```

A few interesting default parameters to look at are the following:

- **Concurrent users**: This specifies the load executed
- **Failures until abort**: This specifies the number of failures that will abort the execution
- **Time to run**: This specifies the amount of out time
- **Repetitions**: This specifies the iterations to perform
- **Resource file**: This specifies the default configuration file

Since the default configuration does not specify the time to run or repetitions, the tool keeps executing until it finds the specified number of failures. You should edit the configuration file specified by the resource file and modify the defaults as per your requirements.

Alternatively, you could pass the parameters from the command line using the available options, for example:

```
$ siege -c 15 -r 10 -q http://192.168.2.100/
```

The preceding command puts a load of 15 users for about 10 iterations. The -q option makes sure that Siege prints only the results and errors (if any).

There are certain parameters that cannot be controlled from the command-line options. The connection timeout is one such parameter. Set the timeout parameter value in the default configuration file located at /etc/siegerc. Since the web server is on the local network, keep the value of the timeout quite low, for example, 5 or 10 seconds. After saving the file, run siege with the -C option to list the configuration. It should list the timeout as follows:

```
CURRENT SIEGE CONFIGURATION
Mozilla/5.0 (unknown-x86_64-linux-gnu) Siege/3.0.9
Edit the resource file to change the settings.
-----------------------------------------------
version:            3.0.9
socket timeout:        10
```

The siege command also defines a behavior for the test's execution. The following are the modes in which Siege can be executed:

- **Default**: This is the default behavior of Siege. Basically, the test hits the URL from all simulated users. For every simulated user, the next hit will come after a default delay of 1 second. The time interval can be changed by modifying the delay property in the configuration file.

- **Benchmark**: In this mode, the test engine neglects the delay and runs as fast as the server and the network allow it to. Every simulated user hits the next URL just after the previous one. Use the -b option to enable this mode of execution; optionally, set the benchmark property to true.

# Siege test results

Before we start analyzing results, we need to make sure that the server is working at its peak. In order to do so, run Siege in benchmark mode with a large user count and with a moderate number of iterations. Alternatively, you could also use the -t option to specify the time frame for which Siege should run. The test should be performed a couple of times, and the results should be averaged to create the metrics.

In order to determine the error rate and the throughput, make sure that we set a value for the timeout. After this, execute Siege with numbers until we start getting an error rate. Also, you need to make sure that Siege does not abort execution due to a large number of errors. If this causes an issue, increase the number of failures to a reasonable number to then arrive at a result. The following code shows this:

```
$ siege -b -c 790 -r 50 -q http://192.168.2.100/hello
```

The preceding code gives the following output:

```
[error] socket: read error Connection reset by peer sock.c:479:
Connection reset by peer
    done.
Transactions:               37164 hits
Availability:               94.09 %
Elapsed time:               14.29 secs
Data transferred:           130.14 MB
Response time:              0.19 secs
Transaction rate:           2600.70 trans/sec
Throughput:                 9.11 MB/sec
Concurrency:                492.12
Successful transactions:    37164
Failed transactions:        2336
Longest transaction:        5.02
Shortest transaction:       0.00
```

In order to determine the response time, run the same test but after removing the timeout set in Siege. The test will execute all transactions without any errors but will have a larger response time. Optionally, we could increase the users a little more and then determine the response time.

The results from Siege can be evaluated to form the metrics as follows:

- **Throughput**: The transaction rate defines this metric, for example, 2600 requests per second
- **Error rate**: Availability defines this metric, for example, 94 percent availability will make the error rate 6 percent
- **Response time**: The results show the response time

# Generating metrics using Apache JMeter

In this section, we will work with Apache JMeter, a free, open source load-testing tool for analyzing and measuring the performance of web applications. JMeter not only simulates the load, but there are numerous response verifications that can be performed. The tool also enables server monitoring and the graphical analysis of results. It can also execute use cases where certain steps need to take place.

JMeter offers the following varied features:

- Loads varied test systems, such as the Web (HTTP/HTTPS), SOAP, FTP, JMS, e-mail (SMTP/POP3/IMAP), native commands, TCP, and so on
- Based on GUI
- Completely based on Java (thus portable across various operating systems)
- Multithreading framework (allows us to simulate concurrent users)
- Used in a distributed manner (simulating loads from different machines simultaneously)
- Large catalog of plugins offering various capabilities
- Offline analysis and replaying of tests

The tool is plugin-based and has a large catalog of existing plugins. It can be extended to perform additional tasks. In short, the tool is a Swiss Army knife for developers, where they can perform different kinds of testing using it.

## Installing JMeter

JMeter is easy to install. It can be downloaded from `http://jmeter.apache.org/`. The site provides an archive in the `.tgz` and `.zip` formats. You can download either of them and extract them to a location. At the time of writing the book, version 2.12 is the latest version available to download.

The extracted archive will have the following structure:

- `bin`: This contains the JMeter executable, examples, and templates.
- `docs`: This contains Javadocs for the JMeter code base
- `extras`: This contains miscellaneous items that are add-ons to JMeter, such as Ant
- `lib`: This contains all the required libraries
- `licenses`: This contains licenses bundled for libraries used in JMeter
- `printable_docs`: This contains the user guide and other help documents
- `README`, `LICENSE`, and `NOTICE` files

Before we can start running JMeter, we need to make sure that Java is available on the box.

# Installing Java

JMeter requires a Java runtime to be available. The runtime version has to be 6 or above. Check whether Java is available using the following code:

```
$ java --version
```

If Java is not available, install the OpenJDK runtime available using `apt-get`:

```
$ sudo apt-get update
$ sudo apt-get install default-jdk
```

 The preceding command installs a default JDK runtime available for your Ubuntu. If you want a specific version, say JDK7 or JDK8, then install the `openjdk-7-jdk` or `openjdk-8-jdk` packages, respectively.

This will install OpenJDK on the box. However, if you want to install Oracle JDK, you have to use the following commands:

```
$ sudo apt-get install python-software-properties
$ sudo add-apt-repository ppa:webupd8team/java
$ sudo apt-get update
```

This will install a third-party `apt-get` repository, from where the package will be installed as Oracle does not provide a repository for this. Now, you can install JDK using the following command:

```
$ sudo apt-get install oracle-java6-installer
```

The preceding command installs Oracle JDK 6. If you want a specific version, say JDK7 or JDK8, then install `oracle-java7-installer` or `oracle-java8-installer` packages, respectively.

# Setting JAVA_HOME

Once a version of Java is installed on the box, you need to set the JAVA_HOME environment variable. This can be done by finding the path of the Java installation and then adding the variable to /etc/environment.

Determine the Java location using update-alternatives as follows:

```
$ sudo update-alternatives --config java
```

This lists all the Java installations available on your box, as shown in the following output:

```
There are 4 choices for the alternative java (providing /usr/bin/java).

  Selection    Path                                            Priority   Status
  ------------------------------------------------------------------------------
    0            /usr/lib/jvm/java-8-oracle/jre/bin/java          1073      auto mode
  * 1            /usr/lib/jvm/java-7-openjdk-amd64/jre/bin/java   1071      manual mode
    2            /usr/lib/jvm/java-8-oracle/jre/bin/java          1073      manual mode
    3            /usr/lib/jvm/jdk1.6.0_45/bin/java               2         manual mode
    4            /usr/lib/jvm/jdk1.7.0_13/bin/java               1         manual mode

Press enter to keep the current choice[*], or type selection number:
```

Copy the path from your preferred installation, and then edit /etc/environment to add JAVA_HOME variable:

```
JAVA_HOME="YOUR_PATH"
```

Now, reload the /etc/environment configuration:

```
$ source /etc/environment
```

Verify the change by executing the following command:

```
echo $JAVA_HOME
```

# Running JMeter

The `bin` folder in the JMeter installation offers all the scripts to run it. The tool can be executed in any of the following modes:

GUI mode:

- To run the JMeter UI, execute `jmeter.sh`, which is available in the `bin` folder under the JMeter installation path. You could do several things there:
    1. Create test plans.
    2. Run the proxy server to record test plans.
    3. Execute test plans.
    4. See the live status of a running test.
    5. Analyze existing results and many more things.

- The UI is quite intuitive; play with it to get to know it better. Going further, we will work in the GUI mode to build test plans and analyze results.

Non-GUI mode:

- JMeter can also be run in a non-UI mode. The tool can run existing test plans and log outputs. This mode is quite helpful when the tool runs in the distributed mode. Run the `jmeter.sh` command with the `-n` and `-t` options. Use the `-l` and `-j` options to specify the files to which the results and JMeter logs are saved. The following code shows this:

```
$ ./jmeter.sh -n -t test-plan -j test.log
```

- In addition to this, the `bin` folder contains the following scripts to control the non-GUI JMeter instance:
    - `shutdown.sh`: This is used to gracefully shut down the non-GUI instance
    - `stoptest.sh`: This is used to abruptly shut down the non-GUI instance

Server mode:

- This mode is used when simulating load from multiple machines. All the machines run a server component by executing the `-s` option or the `jmeter-server.sh` script in the `bin` folder. All these servers are controlled via a master client running the JMeter GUI.

If your network has proxy server settings, then you may want to pass this additional information to the JMeter engine. In order to do so, use the following options:

- -H: This specifies the proxy server hostname or IP address
- -P: This specifies the proxy server port
- -u: This specifies the proxy server username if required
- -a: This specifies the proxy server password if required

# Components of JMeter

JMeter tests are composed of several elements. These elements are responsible for making requests, verifying responses, doing analyses, generating graphs, simulating loads, and so on. Similar types of elements are grouped together to define JMeter components. In the following section, we will discuss the important components required to build a test.

## Threads

This is the starting point of a test. The thread component defines the pool of users that will execute the load in the particular test. The steps that need to be performed are grouped under the threads element. The element provides options to simulate load in various ways, for example, all in one go, increasing with time, and so on. The component also allows you to schedule tests for a later time.

## Sampler

The sampler elements are responsible for making actual requests. JMeter supports loads of protocols, such as FTP, HTTP, JDBC, and so on. There are samplers for each of them. Each sampler provides options to configure the requests that it makes.

## Configuration elements

Configuration elements are used to set up values and variables that can be used by samplers. If the test contains multiple samplers, then instead of setting common values in each of them, add a relevant configuration element.

## Assertions

These are used to verify the validity of the response. Each sample has assertions that perform checks to validate the response received. Unless an assertion is added under the sampler, which would mean it only applies to the particular sampler; it is applicable to all the samplers that are part of the test.

## Listeners

Listeners gather all data from tests. There are various listeners that can analyze the test results and build graphs and tables out of them. All listeners allow us to save data in the CSV or XML format for later reference.

## Test plan

All the preceding elements are grouped together under the test plan element. The plan can set up the variables required in the test. The plans provide additional settings for tests, such as simulating users one by one instead of in parallel, adding JARs to the test's classpath, and so on.

Besides the preceding components, JMeter provides various kinds of components, such as preprocessors, postprocessors, timers, logic controllers, and so on. The chapter only covers the components required to build basic tests.

 For a complete description of the uses of components, refer to the JMeter documentation at `http://jmeter.apache.org/usermanual/`.

# Building JMeter test plans

In order to define a test, we need to build requests and validate and analyze the response received. Instead of adding HTTP request samplers, we can run a proxy server, packed in JMeter, and record all samples.

Let's start building a simple test plan by starting JMeter in GUI mode, as shown here:

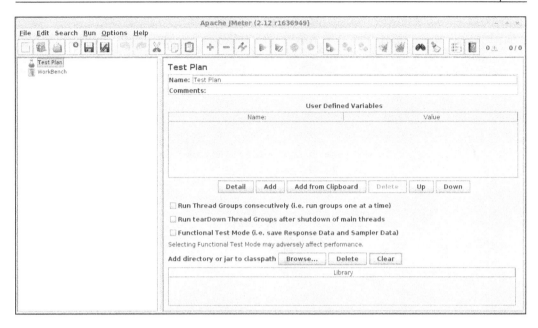

The next step is to start the proxy server and point the browser to it. The option is available under **Workbench**. Navigate to **Workbench** and right-click on **Add | Non Test Elements | HTTP(S) Test Script Recorder**.

Take a note of the port on which the proxy server will run; by default, it will run on `8080`. Click on **Start** to run the server, as shown here:

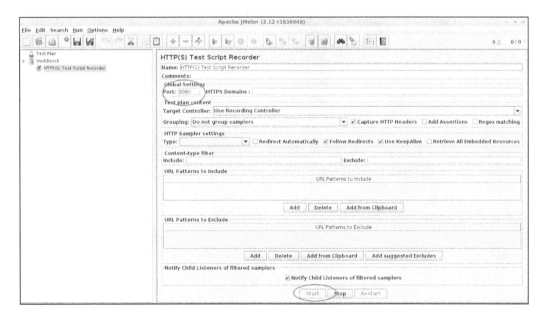

The proxy server is now running on `127.0.0.1:8080`. Apply these settings in your browser under **Network | Settings**. The following screenshot is the result of these steps:

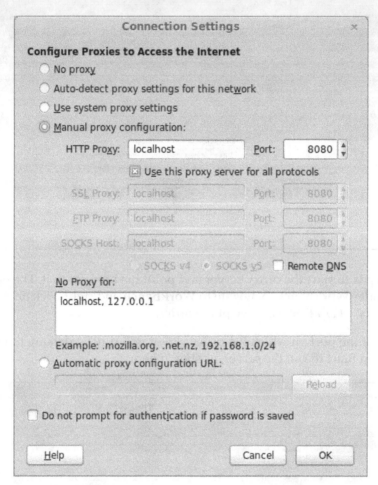

 If you are going to access web pages running on the localhost server, make sure to clear `localhost, 127.0.0.1` from the **No Proxy for** setting.

Now, when you open a web page in the browser, the request will be recorded in JMeter. We will use these recorded requests to generate our test plan.

Access the **Hello world!** page developed in the previous chapter using the IP address of your machine, for example, `http://192.168.2.100/hello/`. This will record requests in the JMeter proxy server, which we will use in our tests.

JMeter tests are grouped as users, so add **Thread Group** under **Test Plan** by navigating to **Test Plan** and right-clicking on **Add | Threads | Thread Group**.

The **Thread Group** element has a couple of useful fields. The fields for **Number of Threads**, **Loop Count**, and **Ramp up Period** can be used to simulate the required load.

Now, select and drag all the requests generated under **HTTP Test Recorder** to **Thread Group**. This adds the selected requests to the test.

The test needs to verify and analyze the responses received for the requests initiated. To see the complete list, navigate to **Thread Group** and right-click on **Add | Assertions**.

For our purposes, we will use the **Response Assertion** component. The panel enables us to compare various fields of the response. Using this, we can verify the response text, response code, response headers, and so on.

Add **Response Assertion** under all requests using the right-click options. In each of the assertions, select **Response Code** and add 200 under **Patterns To Test**.

We need to control timeouts to determine the error rate and the throughput. For each request, JMeter allows us to set a connection timeout and a response timeout. The **HTTP Request** component contains fields for both of these options. Optionally, we could add the **Http Requests Defaults** component available upon navigating to **Thread Group** and right-click on **Add | Config Element**. The values defined in this component will remain the same for all requests. As in Siege, put a small value in the connection timeout as well as the response timeout:

| HTTP Request Defaults |
| --- |
| Name: HTTP Request Defaults |
| Comments: |

Web Server

| Server Name or IP: | | Port Number: | | Timeouts (milliseconds) Connect: 10000 | Response: 30000 |
| --- | --- | --- | --- | --- | --- |

HTTP Request

Implementation: ▼ Protocol [http]: Content encoding:

Path:

Parameters

Send Parameters With the Request:

| Name: | Value | Encode? | Include Equals? |
| --- | --- | --- | --- |

| Detail | Add | Add from Clipboard | Delete | Up | Down |
| --- | --- | --- | --- | --- | --- |

Proxy Server

| Server Name or IP: | | Port Number: | | Username | | Password | |
| --- | --- | --- | --- | --- | --- | --- | --- |

Embedded Resources from HTML Files

☐ Retrieve All Embedded Resources ☐ Use concurrent pool. Size: 4 URLs must match:

Next, to analyze the result, we need to add **Listener** by right-clicking on **Add options on Thread Group**. For our purposes, we will use the **Aggregate Report** component. The component aggregates the response information and provides the request count, minimum, maximum, average, error rate, approximate throughput (request/second), and kilobytes per second for each request.

Along with the **Aggregate Report** component, add the **View Results Tree** component. The component will show all responses in the form of a tree. It also allows you to inspect response codes, the time taken, headers, and so on. The component can selectively show errors, success messages, or all requests. It is quite helpful to get error requests in the component as you can analyze the response to see what has caused the issues.

We are done with all the components that are required; now run the test by clicking on the **Start** button on the toolbar. The toolbar offers handy buttons, such as **Toggle Log Viewer** for error logs and **Clear all** to remove previous results. Also, once the test starts, the tool will enable the **Stop** button to stop the test. Post the test execution, **Aggregate Report** should display the numbers we want to know.

 The default value of one user is too low to generate any kind of useful numbers. To get some actual numbers, increase **Number of threads** to 1,400, **Loop count** to 100 and run the test.

# JMeter test results

During or after test execution, **Aggregate Report** will display the results. The table shows all the metrics that are required to create our baseline. The aggregated response at the bottom is either the sum or the average of different components. We should be looking at the metrics of each request, which will give us more relevant information.

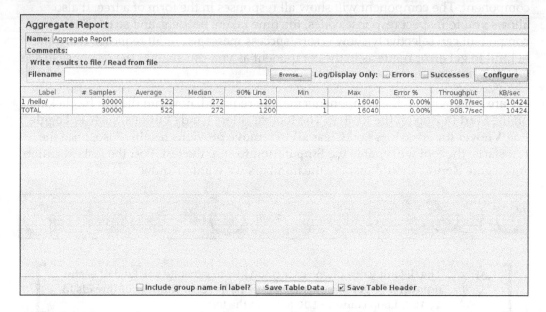

The preceding figure shows the metrics values as follows:

- **Throughput**: 908.7 requests/second.

- **Error rate**: JMeter makes this metric readily available.

- **Response time**: Since the tests are running on the local network, the latency is next to nothing. The average response time is shown as **522** milliseconds.

If there are any errors reported, navigate to the **View Results Tree** component. It will show the error requests in red. Click on any of them to see the response received. If the test contains assertions, then expand the request tree to see the assertions that have failed.

# Summary

In this chapter, you learned about the concepts of performance testing and baselines. Both of these use performance metrics defined by the error rate, throughput, and response time. The chapter gives an overview of some of the tools that can be used by system administrators and developers to determine performance metrics.

One thing to note is that the tools covered in this chapter simulate a browser, but they are not browsers. They do not understand a web page and cannot interpret HTML/JS/CSS. Thus, they cannot determine any errors that people will see when they load the site. The chapter only covers the tools in brief, listing the important features. The aim of this chapter is to enable the reader to generate a baseline that can be compared to determine the optimization done in the upcoming chapters.

In the next chapter, we'll take a look at the NGINX configuration.

# 3
# Tweaking NGINX Configuration

NGINX is fast, but the default configuration is not good enough to take the most out of the underlying hardware. The chapter takes the NGINX configuration built in *Chapter 1, Working with NGINX*, and tunes it to attain optimal performance.

In this chapter, we will cover the following topics:

- NGINX configuration syntax
- Configuring NGINX workers
- Configuring NGINX I/O
- Configuring TCP
- Setting up the server

## NGINX configuration syntax

In *Chapter 1, Working with NGINX*, we got a glimpse of an NGINX configuration. This section aims to cover it in more detail. The complete configuration file has a logical structure that is composed of directives grouped into a number of sections. A section defines the configuration for a particular NGINX module, for example, the `http` section defines the configuration for the `ngx_http_core` module.

An NGINX configuration has the following syntax:

- Valid directives begin with a variable name and then state an argument or series of arguments separated by spaces.

- All valid directives end with a semicolon (;).

- Sections are defined with curly braces ({}).

- Sections can be nested in one another. The nested section defines a module valid under the particular section, for example, the `gzip` section under the `http` section.

- Configuration outside any section is part of the NGINX global configuration.

- The lines starting with the hash (#) sign are comments.

- Configurations can be split into multiple files, which can be grouped using the `include` directive. This helps in organizing code into logical components. Inclusions are processed recursively, an `include` file can also have `include` statements.

- Spaces, tabs, and new line characters are not part of the NGINX configuration. They are not interpreted by the NGINX engine, but they help to make the configuration more readable.

Thus, the complete file looks like the following code:

```
#The configuration begins here
global1 value1;
#This defines a new section
section {
  sectionvar1 value1;
  include file1;
   subsection {
     subsectionvar1 value1;
   }
}
#The section ends here
global2 value2;
# The configuration ends here
```

NGINX provides the `-t` option, which can be used to test and verify the configuration written in the file. If the file or any of the included files contains any errors, it prints the line numbers causing the issue:

```
$ sudo nginx -t
```

This checks the validity of the default configuration file. If the configuration is written in a file other than the default one, use the -c option to test it.

 You cannot test half-baked configurations, for example, you defined a server section for your domain in a separate file. Any attempt to test such a file will throw errors. The file has to be complete in all respects.

Now that we have a clear idea of the NGINX configuration syntax, we will try to play around with the default configuration. This chapter only aims to discuss the parts of the configuration that have an impact on performance.

The NGINX catalog has a large number of modules that can be configured for different purposes. This chapter does not try to cover all of them as the details are beyond the scope of the book. Please refer to the NGINX documentation at `http://nginx.org/en/docs/` to know more about the modules.

# Configuring NGINX workers

NGINX runs a fixed number of worker processes as per the specified configuration. As explained in *Chapter 1*, *Working with NGINX*, these worker processes are responsible for all request processing. In the following sections, we will work with NGINX worker parameters. These parameters are mostly part of the NGINX global context.

## worker_processes

The `worker_processes` directive controls the number of workers:

```
worker_processes 1;
```

The default value for this is 1, which means that NGINX runs only one worker. The value should be changed to an optimal value depending on the number of cores available, disks, network subsystem, server load, and so on.

As a starting point, set the value to the number of cores available. Determine the number of cores available using `lscpu`:

```
$ lscpu
Architecture:      x86_64
CPU op-mode(s):    32-bit, 64-bit
Byte Order:        Little Endian
CPU(s):         4
```

The same can be accomplished by greping out `cpuinfo`:

```
$ cat /proc/cpuinfo | grep 'processor' | wc -l
```

Now, set this value to the parameter:

```
# One worker per CPU-core.
worker_processes 4;
```

Alternatively, the directive can have `auto` as its value. This determines the number of cores and spawns an equal number of workers.

When NGINX is running with SSL, it is a good idea to have multiple workers. SSL handshake is blocking in nature and involves disk I/O. Thus, using multiple workers leads to improved performance.

## accept_mutex

Since we have configured multiple workers in NGINX, we should also configure the flags that impact worker selection. The `accept_mutex` parameter available under the `events` section will enable each of the available workers to accept new connections one by one. By default, the flag is set to `on`. The following code shows this:

```
events {
    accept_mutex on;
}
```

If the flag is turned to `off`, all of the available workers will wake up from the waiting state, but only one worker will process the connection. This results in the *Thundering Herd* phenomenon, which is repeated a number of times per second. The phenomenon causes reduced server performance as all the woken-up workers take up CPU time before going back to the wait state. This results in unproductive CPU cycles and nonutilized context switches.

## accept_mutex_delay

When `accept_mutex` is enabled, only one worker, which has the mutex lock, accepts connections, while others wait for their turn. The `accept_mutex_delay` corresponds to the timeframe for which the worker would wait, and after which it tries to acquire the mutex lock and starts accepting new connections. The directive is available under the `events` section with a default value of 500 milliseconds. The following code shows this:

```
events{
    accept_mutex_delay 500ms;
}
```

# worker_connections

The next configuration to look at is `worker_connections`, with a default value of `512`. The directive is present under the `events` section. The directive sets the maximum number of simultaneous connections that can be opened by a worker process. The following code shows this:

```
events{
    worker_connections 512;
}
```

Increase `worker_connections` to something like 1,024 to accept more simultaneous connections.

> The value of `worker_connections` does not directly translate into the number of clients that can be served simultaneously. Each browser opens a number of parallel connections to download various components that compose a web page, for example, images, scripts, and so on. Different browsers have different values for this, for example, IE works with two parallel connections while Chrome opens six connections. The number of connections also includes sockets opened with the upstream server, if any.

# worker_rlimit_nofile

The number of simultaneous connections is limited by the number of file descriptors available on the system as each socket will open a file descriptor. If NGINX tries to open more sockets than the available file descriptors, it will lead to the `Too many opened files` message in the error.log.

Check the number of file descriptors using `ulimit`:

```
$ ulimit -n
```

Now, increase this to a value more than `worker_process * worker_connections`. The value should be increased for the user that runs the worker process. Check the user directive to get the username.

NGINX provides the `worker_rlimit_nofile` directive, which can be an alternative way of setting the available file descriptor rather modifying `ulimit`. Setting the directive will have a similar impact to updating `ulimit` for the worker user. The value of this directive overrides the `ulimit` value set for the user. The directive is not present by default. Set a large value to handle large simultaneous connections. The following code shows this:

```
worker_rlimit_nofile 20960;
```

> To determine the OS limits imposed on a process, read the file /proc/$pid/limits. $pid corresponds to the PID of the process.

## multi_accept

The `multi_accept` flag enables an NGINX worker to accept as many connections as possible when it gets the notification of a new connection. The purpose of this flag is to accept all connections in the listen queue at once. If the directive is disabled, a worker process will accept connections one by one. The following code shows this:

```
events{
    multi_accept on;
}
```

The directive is available under the `events` section with the default value `off`.

> If the server has a constant stream of incoming connections, enabling `multi_accept` may result in a worker accepting more connections than the number specified in `worker_connections`. The overflow will lead to performance loss as the previously accepted connections, part of the overflow, will not get processed.

## use

NGINX provides several methods for connection processing. Each of the available methods allows NGINX workers to monitor multiple socket file descriptors, when there is data available for reading/writing. These calls allow NGINX to process multiple socket streams without getting stuck in any one of them. The methods are platform-dependent, and the `configure` command, used to build NGINX, selects the most efficient method available on the platform. If we want to use other methods, they must be enabled first in NGINX.

The use directive allows us to override the default method with the method specified. The directive is part of the events section:

```
events {
  use select;
}
```

NGINX supports the following methods of processing connections:

- select: This is the standard method of processing connections. It is built automatically on platforms that lack more efficient methods. The module can be enabled or disabled using the --with-select_module or --without-select_module configuration parameter.

- poll: This is the standard method of processing connections. It is built automatically on platforms that lack more efficient methods. The module can be enabled or disabled using the --with-poll_module or --without-poll_module configuration parameter.

- kqueue: This is an efficient method of processing connections available on FreeBSD 4.1, OpenBSD 2.9+, NetBSD 2.0, and OS X.

  There are the additional directives kqueue_changes and kqueue_events. These directives specify the number of changes and events that NGINX will pass to the kernel. The default value for both of these is 512.

 The kqueue method will ignore the multi_accept directive if it has been enabled.

- epoll: This is an efficient method of processing connections available on Linux 2.6+. The method is similar to the FreeBSD kqueue.

  There is also the additional directive epoll_events. This specifies the number of events that NGINX will pass to the kernel. The default value for this is 512.

- /dev/poll: This is an efficient method of processing connections available on Solaris 7 11/99+, HP/UX 11.22+, IRIX 6.5.15+, and Tru64 UNIX 5.1A+.

  This has the additional directives, devpoll_events and devpoll_changes. The directives specify the number of changes and events that NGINX will pass to the kernel. The default value for both of these is 32.

- eventport: This is an efficient method of processing connections available on Solaris 10. The method requires necessary security patches to avoid kernel crash issues.

- rtsig: Real-time signals is a connection processing method available on Linux 2.2+. The method has some limitations. On older kernels, there is a system-wide limit of 1,024 signals. For high loads, the limit needs to be increased by setting the rtsig-max parameter. For kernel 2.6+, instead of the system-wide limit, there is a limit on the number of outstanding signals for each process. NGINX provides the worker_rlimit_sigpending parameter to modify the limit for each of the worker processes:

```
worker_rlimit_sigpending 512;
```

The parameter is part of the NGINX global configuration.

If the queue overflows, NGINX drains the queue and uses the poll method to process the unhandled events. When the condition is back to normal, NGINX switches back to the rtsig method of connection processing. NGINX provides the rtsig_overflow_events, rtsig_overflow_test, and rtsig_overflow_threshold parameters to control how a signal queue is handled on overflows.

The rtsig_overflow_events parameter defines the number of events passed to poll.

The rtsig_overflow_test parameter defines the number of events handled by poll, after which NGINX will drain the queue.

Before draining the signal queue, NGINX will look up how much it is filled. If the factor is larger than the specified rtsig_overflow_threshold, it will drain the queue.

 The rtsig method requires accept_mutex to be set. The method also enables the multi_accept parameter.

# Configuring NGINX I/O

In *Chapter 1,Working with NGINX*, we discussed the --with-file-aio parameter that can be provided while configuring NGINX, which can enable it to perform asynchronous I/O. Besides this, NGINX can also take advantage of the Sendfile and direct I/O options available in the kernel. In the following sections, we will try to configure parameters available for disk I/O.

# Sendfile

When a file is transferred by an application, the kernel first buffers the data and then sends the data to the application buffers. The application, in turn, sends the data to the destination. The `Sendfile` method is an improved method of data transfer, in which data is copied between file descriptors within the OS kernel space, without transferring data to the application buffers. This results in the improved utilization of the operating system's resources.

The method can be enabled using the `sendfile` directive. The directive is available for the `http`, `server`, and `location` sections:

```
http{
    sendfile on;
}
```

The flag is set to `off` by default.

# Direct I/O

The OS kernel usually tries to optimize and cache any read/write requests. Since the data is cached within the kernel, any subsequent read request to the same place will be much faster because there's no need to read the information from slow disks.

Direct I/O is a feature of the filesystem where reads and writes go directly from the applications to the disk, thus bypassing all OS caches. This results in better utilization of CPU cycles and improved cache effectiveness.

The method is used in places where the data has a poor hit ratio. Such data does not need to be in any cache and can be loaded when required. It can be used to serve large files. The `directio` directive enables the feature. The directive is available for the `http`, `server`, and `location` sections:

```
location /video/ {
    directio 4m;
}
```

Any file that's larger than that specified in the directive will be loaded by direct I/O. The parameter is disabled by default.

 The use of direct I/O to serve a request will automatically disable `Sendfile` for the particular request.

Direct I/O depends on the block size while doing a data transfer. NGINX has the `directio_alignment` directive to set the block size. The directive is present under the `http`, `server`, and `location` sections:

```
location /video/ {
  directio 4m;
  directio_alignment 512;
}
```

The default value of `512` bytes works well for all boxes unless it is running a Linux implementation of XFS. In such an instance, the size should be increased to 4 KB.

# Asynchronous I/O

Asynchronous I/O allows a process to initiate I/O operations without having to block or wait for it to complete.

The `aio` directive is available under the `http`, `server`, and `location` sections of an NGINX configuration. Depending on the section, the parameter will perform asynchronous I/O for the matching requests. The parameter works on Linux kernel 2.6.22+ and FreeBSD 4.3. The following code shows this:

```
location /data {
  aio on;
}
```

By default, the parameter is set to `off`. On Linux, `aio` needs to be enabled with `directio`, while on FreeBSD, `sendfile` needs to be disabled for `aio` to take effect.

 If NGINX has not been configured with the `--with-file-aio` module, any use of the `aio` directive will cause the `unknown directive aio` error.

The directive has a special value of threads, which enables multithreading for send and read operations. The multithreading support is only available on the Linux platform and can only be used with the `epoll`, `kqueue`, or `eventport` methods of processing requests.

In order to use the threads value, configure multithreading in the NGINX binary using the `--with-threads` option. Post this, add a thread pool in the NGINX global context using the `thread_pool` directive. Use the same pool in the `aio` configuration:

```
thread_pool io_pool threads=16;
http{
….....
    location /data{
      sendfile    on;
      aio          threads=io_pool;
    }
}
```

# Mixing them up

The three directives can be mixed together to achieve different objectives on different platforms. The following configuration will use `sendfile` for files that are smaller than what is specified in `directio`. Files served by `directio` will be read using asynchronous I/O:

```
location /archived-data/{
  sendfile on;
  aio on;
  directio 4m;
}
```

The `aio` directive has a `sendfile` value, which is available only on the FreeBSD platform. The value can be used to perform `Sendfile` in an asynchronous manner:

```
location /archived-data/{
  sendfile on;
  aio sendfile;
}
```

NGINX invokes the `sendfile()` system call, which returns with no data in the memory. Post this, NGINX initiates data transfer in an asynchronous manner.

# Configuring TCP

HTTP is an application-based protocol, which uses TCP as the transport layer. In TCP, data is transferred in the form of blocks known as TCP packets. NGINX provides directives to alter the behavior of the underlying TCP stack. These parameters alter flags for an individual socket connection.

## TCP_NODELAY

TCP/IP networks have the "small packet" problem, where single-character messages can cause network congestion on a highly loaded network. Such packets are 41 bytes in size, where 40 bytes are for the TCP header and 1 byte has useful information. These small packets have a huge overhead of around 4000 percent and can saturate a network.

John Nagle solved the problem (Nagle's algorithm) by not sending the small packets immediately. All such packets are collected for a certain amount of time and then sent in one go as a single packet. This results in the improved efficiency of the underlying network. Thus, a typical TCP/IP stack waits for up to 200 milliseconds before sending the data packages to the client.

It is important to note that the problem exists with applications such as Telnet, where each keystroke is sent over wire. The problem is not relevant to a web server, which severs static files. The files will mostly form full TCP packets, which can be sent immediately instead of waiting for 200 milliseconds.

The `TCP_NODELAY` option can be used while opening a socket to disable Nagle's buffering algorithm and send the data as soon as it is available. NGINX provides the `tcp_nodelay` directive to enable this option. The directive is available under the `http`, `server`, and `location` sections of an NGINX configuration:

```
http{
    tcp_nodelay on;
}
```

The directive is enabled by default.

 NGINX use `tcp_nodelay` for connections with the keep-alive mode.

# TCP_CORK

As an alternative to Nagle's algorithm, Linux provides the TCP_CORK option. The option tells the TCP stack to append packets and send them when they are full or when the application instructs to send the packet by explicitly removing TCP_CORK. This results in an optimal amount of data packets being sent and, thus, improves the efficiency of the network. The TCP_CORK option is available as the TCP_NOPUSH flag on FreeBSD and Mac OS.

NGINX provides the tcp_nopush directive to enable TCP_CORK over the connection socket. The directive is available under the http, server, and location sections of an NGINX configuration:

```
http{
  tcp_nopush on;
}
```

The directive is disabled by default.

 NGINX uses tcp_nopush for requests served with sendfile.

# Setting them up

The two directives discussed previously do mutually exclusive things; the former makes sure that the network latency is reduced, while the latter tries to optimize the data packets sent. An application should set both of these options to get efficient data transfer.

Enabling tcp_nopush along with sendfile makes sure that while transferring a file, the kernel creates the maximum amount of full TCP packets before sending them over wire. The last packet(s) can be partial TCP packets, which could end up waiting with TCP_CORK being enabled. NGINX makes sure it removes TCP_CORK to send these packets. Since tcp_nodelay is also set at this point, these packets are immediately sent over the network without any delay.

# Setting up the server

The following configuration sums up all the changes proposed in the preceding sections:

```
worker_processes 3;
worker_rlimit_nofile 8000;

events {
  multi_accept on;
  use epoll;
  worker_connections 1024;
}

http {
  sendfile on;
  aio on;
  directio 4m;
  tcp_nopush on;
  tcp_nodelay on;
  # Rest Nginx configuration removed for brevity
}
```

It is assumed that NGINX runs on a quad core server. Thus, three worker processes have been spanned to take advantage of three out of four available cores and leaving one core for other processes.

Each of the workers has been configured to work with 1,024 connections. Correspondingly, the nofile limit has been increased to 8,000. By default, all worker processes operate with mutex; thus, the flag has not been set. Each worker processes multiple connections in one go using the epoll method.

In the http section, NGINX has been configured to serve files larger than 4 MB using direct I/O, while efficiently buffering smaller files using Sendfile. TCP options have also been set up to efficiently utilize the available network.

# Measuring gains

It is time to test the changes and make sure that they have given performance gain.

Run a series of tests using Siege/JMeter to get new performance numbers. The tests should be performed with the same configuration to get a comparable output:

```
$ siege -b -c 790 -r 50 -q http://192.168.2.100/hello
```

```
Transactions:               79000 hits
Availability:               100.00 %
Elapsed time:               24.25 secs
Data transferred:           12.54 MB
Response time:              0.20 secs
Transaction rate:           3257.73 trans/sec
Throughput:                 0.52 MB/sec
Concurrency:                660.70
Successful transactions:    39500
Failed transactions:        0
Longest transaction:        3.45
Shortest transaction:       0.00
```

The results from Siege should be evaluated and compared to the baseline. The following conclusions are derived while comparing the new numbers with the numbers generated in *Chapter 2, Benchmarking the Server*:

- **Throughput**: The transaction rate defines this as 3250 requests/second
- **Error rate**: Availability is reported as 100 percent; thus; the error rate is 0 percent
- **Response time**: The results show a response time of 0.20 seconds

Thus, these new numbers demonstrate performance improvement in various respects.

 After the server configuration is updated with all the changes, reperform all tests with increased numbers. The aim should be to determine the new baseline numbers for the updated configuration.

# Summary

The chapter started with an overview of the NGINX configuration syntax. Going further, we discussed `worker_connections` and the related parameters. These allow you to take advantage of the available hardware. The chapter also talked about the different event processing mechanisms available on different platforms. The configuration discussed helped in processing more requests, thus improving the overall throughput.

NGINX is primarily a web server; thus, it has to serve all kinds of static content. Large files can take advantage of direct I/O, while smaller content can take advantage of `Sendfile`. The different disk modes make sure that we have an optimal configuration to serve the content.

In the TCP stack, we discussed the flags available to alter the default behavior of the TCP sockets. The `tcp_nodelay` directive helps in improving latency. The `tcp_nopush` directive can help in efficiently delivering the content. Both these flags lead to improved response time.

In the last part of the chapter, we applied all the changes to our server and then did performance tests to determine the effectiveness of the changes done. In the next chapter, we will try to configure buffers, timeouts, and compression to improve the utilization of the available network.

# 4
# Controlling Buffers, Timeouts, and Compression

So far, we have built an NGINX configuration to make the best use of the available platform. This is just one part of the story where we have optimized NGINX request processing. We can also customize various client-side parameters to better utilize the available network, thus increasing the throughput.

In this chapter, we will cover the following topics:

- Configuring buffers
- Configuring timeouts
- Compression
- Controlling logs
- Setting up the server

## Configuring buffers

Request buffers serve an important role in NGINX request handling. On receiving a request, NGINX writes it to these buffers. The data in these buffers is available as NGINX variables, such as $request\_body. If the buffers are small in comparison to the request size, the data gets written to files on the disk and, thus, would involve I/O. NGINX provides various directives that can alter request buffers.

# client_body_buffer_size

This directive sets the buffer size used for the request body. If the body exceeds the buffer size, either the complete body or a part of it gets written to a temporary file. This directive gets ignored if NGINX is configured to use files instead of the memory buffer. By default, the directive sets an 8k buffer for 32-bit systems and a 16k buffer for 64-bit systems. The directive is available under the http, server, and location sections of an NGINX configuration. Here's an example:

```
server{
    client_body_buffer_size 8k;
}
```

# client_max_body_size

This directive sets the maximum request body size handled by NGINX. If the request is larger than the specified size, then NGINX sends back the HTTP 413 (Request Entity too large) error. The directive is of importance if the server handles large file uploads.

By default, the directive sets 1m as the maximum limit. This directive is available under the http, server, and location sections of an NGINX configuration. Here's an example:

```
server{
    client_max_body_size 2m;
}
```

# client_body_in_file_only

This directive disables NGINX buffers and stores the request body in a temporary file. The file contains data as plain text. The directive is available under the http, server, and location sections of an NGINX configuration. It can have one of the following three values:

- off: The value will disable file writing.
- clean: The request body will be written to a file. The file will be removed after processing the request.
- on: The request body will be written to a file. The file will not be removed after processing the request.

By default, the directive is set to `off`. Here's an example:

```
http{
    client_body_in_file_only clean;
}
```

 This directive is quite helpful for debugging purposes. It is not recommended for production deployments.

# client_body_in_single_buffer

This directive instructs NGINX to store the complete request body in a single buffer. By default, the directive is set to `off`. If enabled, it optimizes I/O while reading the `$request_body` variable. The directive is available under the `http`, `server`, and `location` sections of an NGINX configuration. Here's an example:

```
server{
    client_body_in_single_buffer on;
}
```

# client_body_temp_path

This directive specifies the location to store temporary files for the request body. In addition to the location, the directive can also specify whether the files need a folder hierarchy up to three levels. The level is specified as the number of digits used to generate the folder.

By default, NGINX creates temporary files in the `client_body_temp` folder under the NGINX installation path. The directive is available under the `http`, `server`, and `location` sections of an NGINX configuration. Here's an example:

```
server{
    client_body_temp_pathtemp_files 1 2;
    }
```

This directive will generate paths, such as `temp_files/1/05/0000003051`, under the NGINX prefix location.

# client_header_buffer_size

This directive is similar to `client_body_buffer_size`. It allocates a buffer for request headers. If the request header does not fit into a specified buffer, the `large_client_header_buffers` directive is used to allocate a bigger buffer.

The default value of `1k` is good enough for all intents and purposes. This directive is available under the `http` and `server` sections of an NGINX configuration:

```
http{
    client_header_buffer_size 1m;
    }
```

# large_client_header_buffers

This directive specifies the maximum number and size of buffers used for reading large client request headers. These buffers are allocated on demand only when the default buffers are insufficient. The buffers are released when the request is processed or the connection gets transitioned into the keep-alive state.

The default values of `4k` and `8k` buffers are good enough for all intents and purposes. The directive is available under the `http` and `server` sections of an NGINX configuration:

```
http{
    large_client_header_buffers 4 8k;
    }
```

If the request URI exceeds the size of a single buffer, NGINX sends back the `HTTP 414 (Request URI Too Long)` error to the client. Also, if any request header field exceeds the size of a single buffer, NGINX sends back the `HTTP 400 (Bad Request)` error to the client.

# Configuring timeouts

Every request served by NGINX goes through various timeouts. These timeouts, if optimized, can have a considerable impact on the server's performance. Post timeout, the resources are released and, thus, can be utilized for other requests. In the following section, we will configure various timeout directives provided by NGINX.

# keepalive

HTTP is a stateless, request-response-based protocol, where the client opens a TCP connection with the server, sends the request, receives the response, and then the server closes the connection to release the resources.

Now, if the client makes multiple requests to the server, for every request, the client opens a connection, transfers the data, and then the connection is closed by the server. This is quite inefficient if the web pages contain a lot of resources as the browser will open a connection for every resource.

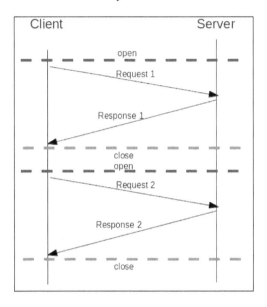

HTTP has the keepalive mode, which instructs the server to hold a TCP connection open once the request has been completed. If the client needs to make another request, it can use this idle keepalive connection rather than creating a new TCP connection. Such a connection can be terminated when the client feels it is no longer required or the server determines that there been no activity over the connection for a certain interval of time (timeout). Modern browsers usually open multiple keepalive connections and use them to serve content.

Since keepalive connections are kept open for an interval of time they have a cost of increased resource utilization. The keepalive timeout should be optimal depending on your website and traffic load. This will improve the site's performance. If the timeout is quite large, then it can have a negative impact on performance during high traffic loads.

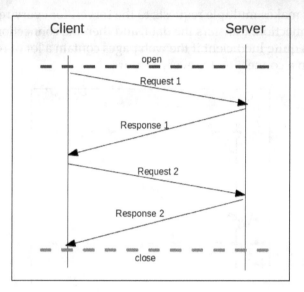

NGINX has a couple of directives to configure keepalive connections.

## keepalive_timeout

This directive configures the timeout for keepalive connections. By default, the value is set to 75 seconds. The value 0 disables keepalive connections. The directive is available under the http, server, and location sections of an NGINX configuration. Here's an example:

```
http{
    keepalive_timeout 20s;
    }
```

This directive also has a second optional time argument, which it sends back in the `Keep-Alive: timeout=time` response header field. The header field is recognized by certain browsers, such as Mozilla, Konqueror, and so on, and could have a different value compared to the timeout. Here's an example:

```
http{
    keepalive_timeout 20s 18s;
    }
$ curl -I http://192.168.2.100/hello
…......
Connection: keep-alive
Keep-Alive: timeout=18
…....
```

## keepalive_requests

This directive configures the total number of requests allowed over a keepalive connection. After the maximum number of requests are made, the server closes the connection.

By default, the directive sets `100` as the maximum number of allowed requests. The directive is available under the `http`, `server`, and `location` sections of an NGINX configuration. Here's an example:

```
http{
    keepalive_requests 20;
    }
```

## keepalive_disable

This directive disables keepalive connections for a particular set of browsers.

By default, the directive sets `msie6` as a value. This directive is available under the `http`, `server`, and `location` sections of an NGINX configuration. Here's an example:

```
http{
    keepalive_disabled msie6 safari;
    }
```

# send_timeout

This directive sets a timeout for transmitting data to the client. This timeout does not apply to the entire transfer but only between two successive write operations. If the timeout expires, NGINX will close the connection.

By default, the directive sets the value as 60 seconds. The directive is available under the `http`, `server`, and `location` sections of an NGINX configuration. Here's an example:

```
server{
    send_timeout 30s;
    }
```

# client_body_timeout

This directive sets a timeout to send the request body from the client. The timeout does not apply to the complete request body but only to two successive read operations. If the client does not send anything within the set time interval, NGINX sends back the `HTTP 408(Request Timed Out)` error.

By default, this directive sets the value as 60 seconds. The directive is available under the `http`, `server`, and `location` sections of an NGINX configuration. Here's an example:

```
server{
    client_body_timeout 30s;
    }
```

# client_header_timeout

The directive sets a timeout to send the complete request header from the client. If the client does not send the complete header information within the set time interval, NGINX sends back the `HTTP 408(Request Timed Out)` error.

By default, the directive sets the value 60 seconds. The directive is available under the `http` and `server` sections of the NGINX configuration. Here's an example:

```
server{
    client_header_timeout 30s;
    }
```

# Compression

Compression can improve website speed by reducing the amount of data transferred over the network. NGINX offers a couple of alternatives to use for serving compressed content.

# ngx_http_gzip_module

This module enables `gzip` compression in NGINX. The server compresses the data and then sends it over wire. Compression is mostly helpful in serving textual content. It does not help in serving noncompressible content, such as JPEG, GIF, MP3, and so on. Also, if the compression level is high, there is not much gain in terms of the compressed data size, and the server mostly ends up wasting CPU cycles.

The module offers the following directives to configure the `gzip` compression.

## gzip

This directive enables `gzip` compression in NGINX. By default, the directive is set to `off`. This directive is available under the `http`, `server`, `location`, and `if` (in the `location` section) sections of an NGINX configuration. Here's an example:

```
http{
    gzip on;
    }
```

## gzip_comp_level

This directive sets a `gzip` compression level of response. The directive has values in the range `1` to `9`. Very high compression will not yield good results as it takes more CPU cycles without much benefit in compressing the data size.

By default, the directive is set to `1`. The values from `1` to `3` offer optimal results as they offer a fine balance between the final compressed sizes and the time spent. This directive is available under the `http`, `server`, and `location` sections of an NGINX configuration. Here's an example:

```
http{
    gzip_comp_level 2;
    }
```

# gzip_min_length

This directive sets the minimum response length that will be compressed. The module determines the response length from the **Content-Length** response header field.

By default, this directive is set to 20 bytes. The directive is available under the http, server, and location sections of an NGINX configuration. Here's an example:

```
http{
    gzip_min_length 1000;
    }
```

# gzip_types

This directive sets the response types that will be compressed. By default, the directive is set to text/html. The directive is available under the http, server, and location sections of an NGINX configuration. Here's an example:

```
http{
    gzip_types text/xml text/css text/plain;
    }
```

 Responses of the text/html type are always compressed. The directive specifies MIME types additional to text/html.

# gzip_proxied

The directive can be used to enable/disable compression if NGINX serves a response via an upstream. The directive can take one or more of the following values to determine what kind of response should be compressed:

- expired: This enables compression if the **Expires** header field has a value to disable caching.

- no-cache/no-store/private: This enables compression if the **Cache-Control** header field has the values no-cache, no-store, or private.

- no_last_modified: This enables compression if the header does not have the **Last-modified** field.

- auth: This enables compression if the header has the **Authorization** field.

- no_etag: This enables compression if the header does not have the **Etag** field.

- any/off: This enables/disables compression for all requests.

By default, the directive is set to off. The directive is available under the http, server, and location sections of an NGINX configuration. Here's an example:

```
http{
    gzip_proxied expired no-cache no-store;
    }
```

# gzip_http_version

The directive sets the minimum HTTP version of a request for a compressed response. By default, the directive sets the value 1.1. The directive is available under the http, server, and location sections of an NGINX configuration. Here's an example:

```
http{
    gzip_http_version 1.1;
    }
```

# gzip_vary

If gzip is enabled, this directive adds the **Vary: Accept-Encoding** header field to the response. The directive is disabled (off) by default. It is available under the http, server, and location sections of an NGINX configuration. Here's an example:

```
http{
    gzip_vary on;
    }
```

# gzip_disable

There are browsers (for example, IE6) that cannot understand gzip compression. This directive can be used in such situations to disable compression by looking into the **User-Agent** request header field.

By default, this directive is not present. The directive is available under the http, server, and location sections of an NGINX configuration. Here's an example:

```
http{
    gzip_disable "MSIE [1-6]\.";
    }
```

# ngx_http_gzip_static_module

This module enables NGINX to serve a precompressed `.gz` extension file instead of a regular file. The server does not generate the `.gz` compressed file; instead, it just tries to send an already existing `.gz` extension file first, if found. This has the benefit of saving server CPU cycles while serving compressed data.

The module is not enabled by default. It can be enabled by passing the `--with-http_gzip_static_module` option while configuring an NGINX binary.

## gzip_static

This directive enables NGINX to send precompressed files with the `.gz` extension. By default, the directive is set to `off`. This directive can be set to `on` where NGINX will determine whether the client supports the `.gz` file; if so, it will send the `.gz` file; otherwise, it will send the regular file. Alternatively, the value can be set to `always`, where NGINX will skip the client check and will serve the request with a `.gz` file, if one exists.

This directive takes into account the values of the `gzip_http_version`, `gzip_proxied`, and `gzip_disable` directives in order to determine whether or not the client supports compressed responses. The directive is available under the http, `server`, and `location` sections of an NGINX configuration. Here's an example:

```
server{
    gzip_static always;
    }
```

# ngx_http_gunzip_module

This module enables NGINX to serve a decompressed response for clients that do not support `gzip` encoding. The module is often used with `ngx_http_gzip_static_module`. NGINX can serve precompressed `.gz` files using `ngx_http_gzip_static_module`. If the client cannot handle compressed responses, then `ngx_http_gunzip_module` can decompress the `.gz` file to serve the request.

This module is not enabled by default. It can be enabled by passing the `--with-http_gunzip_module` option while configuring an NGINX binary.

# gunzip

This directive enables the decompression of `.gz` responses in NGINX. By default, the directive is set to `off`. This directive is available under the `http`, `server`, and `location` sections of an NGINX configuration:

```
location / {
    gzip_static always;
    gunzip on;
    }
```

# Configuring logs

Logging is a double-edged sword. On the one hand, it offers all kinds of useful information, but on the other hand, it has a computational cost. If the application generates thousands of log lines, the cost will have a negative impact on performance. In the following section, we will discuss NGINX directives that can be used to tweak logs.

# access_log

This directive configures logging for all requests served by NGINX. The directive takes multiple parameters that can be used to configure the log path, format template, buffers, and so on. The syslog value can be used to direct logs to a syslog server rather than to a log file. Alternatively, the complete logging can be disabled using `off` as a value.

By default, access logs are enabled to write to the `log/access.log` file in the prespecified combined format. This directive is available under the `limit_except`, `http`, `server`, `location`, and `if` (in location section) sections of an NGINX configuration. Here's an example:

```
http{
    access_log logs/access.log combined;
    }
```

 NGINX sections can contain multiple `access_log` directives specifying different log destinations and, optionally, different format templates.

# log_format

This directive can be used to define a template for the `access_log` directive. The log format can contain any of the existing variables defined in NGINX. By default, NGINX defines the combined format, which it uses in the access log directive. The directive is only available under the `http` section of an NGINX configuration. Here's an example:

```
log_format combined '$remote_addr - $remote_user [$time_local] '
                '"$request" $status $body_bytes_sent '
            '"$http_referer" "$http_user_agent"';
```

# log_subrequest

This directive enables the logging of subrequests in the access log directive. By default, the directive is set to `off`. This directive can be used to enable logging under the `http`, `server`, and `location` sections of an NGINX configuration. Here's an example:

```
http{
    log_subrequest on;
    }
```

# error_log

This directive can be used to configure logging in NGINX. Logs can be directed to a file or the error stream (`stderr`) or to a `syslog` server. The directive also defines a level of logging, namely `debug`, `info`, `notice`, `warn`, `error`, `crit`, `alert`, or `emerg`. Log statements with more severity than configured are logged to the specified destination.

By default, error logs are enabled, with the `error` level, to write to the `log/error.log` file. This directive is available under the `global`, `http`, `server`, and `location` sections of an NGINX configuration. Here's an example:

```
http{
    error_log logs/warn.log warn;
    }
```

NGINX sections can contain multiple `error_log` directives specifying different log destinations and, optionally, different log levels.

# log_not_found

This directive enables/disables the reporting of files not found (HTTP 404 errors) in the error log. By default, the directive is set to on. The directive can be used to enable logging under the `http`, `server`, and `location` sections of an NGINX configuration. Here's an example:

```
http{
    log_not_found on;
    }
```

# Setting up the server

The following configuration sums up all the changes proposed in the preceding sections:

```
http {
  #####
  # Configuring Buffers
  #####
  client_body_buffer_size 15K;
  client_max_body_size 8m;

  #####
  # Configuring Timeouts
  #####
  keepalive_timeout 20;
  client_body_timeout 15;
  client_header_timeout 15;
  send_timeout 10;

  #####
  # Configuring Gzip
  #####
  gzip on;
  gzip_comp_level 2;
  gzip_min_length 1000;
  gzip_proxied any;
  gzip_types text/plain text/css application/json application/x-
  javascript text/xml application/xml application/xml+rss text/
  javascript;
```

```
    #####
# Configuring Logs
    #####
access_log off;
log_not_found off;
error_log logs/error.log crit;

    # Rest NGINX configuration removed for brevity
}
```

The following things are done by the preceding configuration:

- Timeouts are lowered for keepalive, send, and client requests
- Buffers are configured for the request body
- Header buffers are not changed as the defaults are good enough
- Text requests, such as CSS, JS, XML, and so on, are served using Gzip compression
- Logs are kept to a bare minimum

# Measuring gains

It's time to test the changes and make sure that they give a performance gain.

If we try to test the changes using Siege / JMeter, the results do not show any change:

```
$ siege -b -c 790 -r 50 -q http://192.168.2.100/hello
```

```
Transactions:              79000 hits
Availability:              100.00 %
Elapsed time:              24.25 secs
Data transferred:          13.54 MB
Response time:             0.20 secs
Transaction rate:          3268.73 trans/sec
Throughput:                0.52 MB/sec
Concurrency:               642.70
Successful transactions:   39500
Failed transactions:       0
Longest transaction:       3.48
Shortest transaction:      0.00
```

So, did the changes make an impact?

It is important to note here that the changes made in the chapter affect the client that is not running on the same network. Basically, the configured timeouts do not come into play when testing on a fast local network. The timeouts have an effect while testing the pages on the Internet or on a slow network. Thus, a proper environment should be simulated in order to test pages. To test the changes, we deployed pages on an Amazon EC2 server and then tested it.

In order to determine performance numbers for the preceding changes, we need to enable/disable compression and keepalive in our benchmarking tools.

Siege allows us to configure keepalive and compression through the `siegerc` configuration file.

- Disable keeplive by setting the `close` value in the `connection` property
- Disable `gzip` compression by setting the `accept-encoding` property to `identity`

Run a few tests to get some numbers:

```
$ siege -b -c 150 -r 50 -q http://my.server.org/hello
   done.
```

```
Transactions:              15000 hits
Availability:              100.00 %
Elapsed time:              172.72 secs
Data transferred:          3.56 MB
Response time:             1.47 secs
Transaction rate:          86.85 trans/sec
Throughput:                0.02 MB/sec
Concurrency:               127.38
Successful transactions:   15000
Failed transactions:       0
Longest transaction:       13.02
Shortest transaction:      0.65
```

Now, enable both the preceding settings by configuring the `connection` property to `keep-alive` and configuring the `accept-encoding` property to `gzip`. Run a few tests to determine the impact of the changes made:

```
$ siege -b -c 150 -r 50 -q http://my.server.org/hello
    done.
```

```
Transactions:                  15000 hits
Availability:                  100.00 %
Elapsed time:                  55.62 secs
Data transferred:              2.93 MB
Response time:                 0.50 secs
Transaction rate:              269.69 trans/sec
Throughput:                    0.05 MB/sec
Concurrency:                   134.48
Successful transactions:       15000
Failed transactions:           0
Longest transaction:           2.58
Shortest transaction:          0.37
```

A comparison of the two results leads to the following conclusions:

- The throughput has improved significantly from 87 requests/second to 270 requests/sec
- The response time has decreased significantly from 1.47 seconds to 0.5 seconds

In order to run benchmarks with JMeter, we need to configure it in the following manner:

- Disable keepalive by deselecting the **Use Keepalive** checkbox under the HTTP Request configuration element
- Disable `gzip` by setting `identity` in the **Accept Encoding** headers under HTTP Header Manager

Run a few tests to determine some performance numbers. Now, enable the settings by selecting the **Use Keepalive** checkbox and setting the `gzip` value in the **Accept-Encoding** field. Again, run a few tests and compare the results.

# Summary

This chapter was aimed at tweaking an NGINX configuration for HTTP clients. It started with a discussion about NGINX client buffers and related directives. These directives enable limiting I/O while reading requests. The section after that was aimed at the timeouts available in NGINX. It gave insights into the benefits of the keepalive HTTP mode. The sections about compression showed the NGINX configuration to reduce data sent over the network by using gzip in various ways. The chapter also talked about ways to configure NGINX logs and request access logs to control the information logged.

The last section summed up all the required changes and tried to test them. The changes do not yield any gain on a fast network. These configuration changes are aimed at solving issues that manifest on a slow network, and, thus, to test these changes, a proper environment is required.

The directives configured can be readily used by a browser, but the benchmark tooling needs to be configured properly to make use of these settings. The chapter showed ways to enable/disable the required settings in Siege and JMeter. In the end, performance tests were performed to determine the effectiveness of the changes.

In the next chapter, we will try to tune the TCP stack for optimal performance.

# 5
# Configuring the Network Stack

HTTP is a TCP/IP-based system; therefore, an administrator trying to extract the last drop of performance will not only optimize the web server, but also look at the TCP network stack. TCP has various network congestion avoidance defaults, which can be tweaked to yield better bandwidth utilization. Moreover, TCP connections consume server resources, such as ports and memory. These are fixed resources and are only reused when released by previous TCP connections. System administrators can configure parameters for the optimal reuse of these fixed resources.

In this chapter, we will cover the following topics:

- TCP buffers
- TCP states
- Raising server limits
- Setting up the server

The chapter will discuss various commands to tweak TCP parameters on the Debian platform. These commands may vary on other platforms, so please check the related reference documentation.

## TCP buffers

The TCP protocol uses the socket interface to communicate. Its performance does not depend only on network transfer rate, but rather on the product of the transfer rate and the roundtrip time. This is known as the **bandwidth delay product (BDP)**. The BDP measures the amount of data that fills the TCP pipe.

Internally, the OS kernel attaches certain (received and sent) buffers to each of the opened sockets. Each of these buffers must be large enough to hold the TCP data along with an OS-specific overhead. The BDP signifies the buffer space required by the sender and the receiver to obtain maximum throughput on TCP. The send and receive buffers describe a congestion window for a socket communication, which determines how many packets can be sent over the wire in one go. The buffers can be configured to push more network packets over high-speed networks.

The buffer size is limited by the operating system, which imposes an upper bound on the maximum amount of memory available for use by a TCP connection, inclusive of everything. These limits are too small for today's high-speed networks.

The `ping` command can be used to derive the BDP for a network. It gives the roundtrip time, which is multiplied by the network capacity to define the buffer size. Here's the command:

```
buffer size = network capacity * round trip time
```

For example, if the ping time is 30 milliseconds and the network consists of 1G Ethernet, then the buffers should be as follows:

```
.03 sec * (1024 Megabits)*(1/8)= 3.84 MegaBytes
```

The memory consumed by TCP can be found by listing the `net.ipv4.tcp_mem` key using the `sysctl` command:

```
$ sysctl net.ipv4.tcp_mem
net.ipv4.tcp_mem = 188319 251092 376638
```

The output lists three values, namely, minimum, initial, and maximum buffer size.

There is no need to manually tune the values of `tcp_mem`. Since version 2.6.17, the Linux kernel comes bundled with an auto-tuning feature that configures the buffer values dynamically within the specified range. List `net.ipv4.tcp_moderate_rcvbuf` to check for auto-tuning:

```
$ sysct lnet.ipv4.tcp_moderate_rcvbuf
net.ipv4.tcp_moderate_rcvbuf = 1
```

The value 1 indicates that tuning is enabled.

In addition to the total TCP buffer, we can also list the receive and send buffers using the following keys:

- `net.ipv4.tcp_rmem`

    This lists the memory for the TCP receive buffers

- `net.ipv4.tcp_wmem`

    This lists the memory for the TCP send buffers

The keys output three values, namely, minimum, initial, and maximum, for the respective buffers.

The initial size determines the amount of memory allocated at the start, when the socket is created. This should be kept low; otherwise, under heavy traffic conditions, each socket will start allocating large initial memory, which can cause the system to run out of memory, thus yielding poor performance. The Linux kernel's auto-tuning will dynamically adjust the buffers during usage for optimal performance and memory utilization.

The maximum size for the receive and send buffers can be determined using the `net.core.rmem_max` and `net.core.wmem_max` properties. The default values for these properties are quite low — around 200 Kb. Here's an example:

```
$ sysctl net.ipv4.tcp_moderate_rcvbuf
net.core.rmem_max = 212992
$ sysctl net.ipv4.tcp_moderate_rcvbuf
net.core.wmem_max = 212992
```

Using the preceding set of kernel properties, TCP defines what are known as the "receiver window size" and the "sender window size", respectively. Now, if the receiver window is small, then the sender cannot send more data, thus leading to suboptimal performance. Even while sending data, if the "send window" is small, then the server will send smaller data than what the receiver can hold.

Modify these values to something like 16 MB as the maximum window size. Also, modify the maximum values of `net.ipv4.tcp_rmem` and `net.ipv4.tcp_wmem` to the corresponding values. The values can be updated by setting the correct set of keys and values in the `sysctl` command:

```
$ sudo sysctl -w net.core.rmem_max=16777216
net.core.rmem_max = 16777216

$ sudo sysctl -w net.ipv4.tcp_rmem='4096 87380 16777216'
net.ipv4.tcp_rmem = 4096 87380 16777216
```

```
$ sudo sysctl -w net.core.wmem_max=16777216
net.core.wmem_max = 16777216


$ sudo sysctl -w net.ipv4.tcp_wmem='4096 16384 16777216'
net.ipv4.tcp_wmem = 4096 16384 16777216
```

# The TCP window

The TCP header contains a `window` field, which determines the receiver buffer size. The default size of this window is 16 bits, which means it can represent data of a few Kb.

TCP defines a window-scaling option, which can extend the 16-bit TCP window field (part of the TCP header) to 32 bits, essentially allowing larger data packets. The option specifies the count of bits by which the header needs to be shifted. This shifting allows larger values to be sent using the window field. The following diagram shows this:

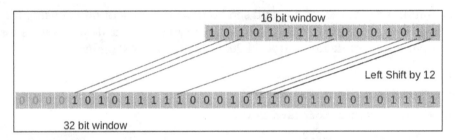

The buffer allocated at the receiving end is dynamically altered by the value in this window field. Window scaling is part of the TCP handshake and is enabled by default. This feature of TCP can be toggled using `net.ipv4.tcp_window_scaling`.

Along with TCP window scaling, the TCP header also defines a timestamp (`net.ipv4.tcp_timestamps`) used to sync packets and a sack (`net.ipv4.tcp_sack`) used to selectively identify packets lost during transmission.

TCP enables all the features mentioned earlier by default. They should not be disabled as turning them off will hurt performance rather than make any gains.

| Source Port | | | Destination Port | |
|---|---|---|---|---|
| Sequence Number | | | | |
| Acknowledgment Number | | | | |
| Offset | Reserved | TCP Flags | Window | |
| Checksum | | | Urgent pointer | |
| TCP Options<br>( No Op, Window Scale, Timestamp, Sack etc.) | | | | Padding |
| Data | | | | |
| **32 bit TCP Header** | | | | |

# TCP control algorithms

TCP uses control algorithms to avoid congestion. There are various implementations for these algorithms. The Linux kernel packs the `htcp`, `cubic`, and `reno` implements. These can be found using the `net.ipv4.tcp_available_congestion_control` key as follows:

```
$ sysctl net.ipv4.tcp_available_congestion_control

net.ipv4.tcp_available_congestion_control = cubic reno
```

> If certain implementations are missing, then you could easily install them using mprobe. The implementations are mostly available as reloadable kernel modules. You can use the following mprobe commands:
>
> ```
> $ sudo modprobetcp_htcp
> $ sudo modprobetcp_bic
> ```

The `reno` implementation has been the classical model of congestion control. It suffers from various issues, for example, it is slow to start. Thus, it is not suitable for high bandwidth networks. `Cubic` has replaced `reno` as the default implementation for various OS kernels.

You can verify the congestion control algorithm used by TCP by listing the `net.ipv4.tcp_congestion_control` key:

```
$ sysctl net.ipv4.tcp_congestion_control

net.ipv4.tcp_congestion_control = cubic
```

# TCP states

A TCP connection usually goes through a series of states during its lifetime. The state signifies the status of the TCP connection. In order to determine the connection state, execute the netstat command:

```
$ sudo netstat --tcp --all --numeric
Active Internet connections (servers and established)
Proto Recv-Q Send-Q Local Address    Foreign Address      State    tcp
0    0 0 0.0.0.0:3306     0.0.0.0:*      LISTEN   tcp    0    0 0.0.0.0:139
0.0.0.0:*      LISTEN
tcp    0    0 192.168.2.111:39551    182.19.89.106:80      ESTABLISHED
tcp    396    0 192.168.2.111:18358    173.194.36.70:443      TIME_WAIT
tcp    0    0 127.0.0.1:80     127.0.0.1:48234    TIME_WAIT
```

The states can contain any of the following values:

- LISTEN: This indicates that the socket is ready for incoming connections
- SYN_SENT: This indicates that the socket is attempting to establish a connection
- SYN_RECV: This indicates that the server has received a connection request
- ESTABLISHED: This indicates that the server has established a connection
- LAST_ACK: This indicates that the server is waiting for ACK as the socket is closed
- CLOSE_WAIT: This indicates that the server is waiting for the socket to close as the client has closed the connection
- TIME_WAIT: This indicates that the server has closed the socket but is waiting for packets in the network
- FIN_WAIT1: This indicates that the connection is shutting down as the socket is closed
- FIN_WAIT2: This indicates that the connection is closed and the socket is waiting for shutdown from client
- CLOSED: This indicates that the socket is not being used

When a TCP connection closes, the connection moves to the TIME_WAIT state. The connection remains in this state for a long period of time, usually twice the maximum segment life (msl). The reason for waiting is that packets may arrive out of order or be retransmitted after the connection has been closed. Thus, the connection is being kept around so that these delayed packets can be handled appropriately.

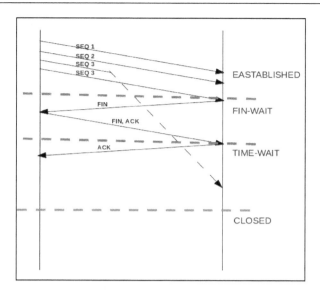

The long TIME_WAIT state results in the memory and ports getting blocked by closed connections. Thus, a heavily loaded server can run out of resources, which can be caused by a large number of connections in the TIME_WAIT state.

The default MSL is 60 seconds, thus making the TIME_WAIT state last for 2 minutes for each closed socket. The MSL can be listed for the net.ipv4.tcp_fin_timeout key:

```
$ sysctl net.ipv4.tcp_fin_timeout
net.ipv4.tcp_fin_timeout = 60
```

To make the TIME_WAIT state last for 40 seconds, decrease the value of net.ipv4. tcp_fin_timeout to 20 seconds:

```
$ sudo sysctl -w net.ipv4.tcp_fin_timeout = 20
net.ipv4.tcp_fin_timeout = 20
```

Another way of improving the utilization of TCP sockets is to configure the TCP behavior using tcp_tw_reuse. The property allows TCP to reuse the TIME_WAIT socket when it is safe from the protocol viewpoint. The configuration is disabled by default; enable it by setting the net.ipv4.tcp_rw_reuse key:

```
$ sysctl net.ipv4.tcp_tw_reuse
net.ipv4.tcp_tw_reuse = 0


$ sudo sysctl -w net.ipv4.tcp_tw_reuse = 1
net.ipv4.tcp_tw_reuse = 1
```

The kernel also presents the `tcp_tw_recycle` option as an alternative to `tcp_tw_reuse`. The `tcp_tw_recycle` option is a more aggressive version of `tcp_tw_reuse` and enables fast recycling of `TIME_WAIT` connections:

```
$ sysctl net.ipv4.tcp_tw_recycle
net.ipv4.tcp_tw_recycle = 0
```

It is not recommended that you enable this option as the kernel makes assumptions before determining whether to reuse a socket. These assumptions can pose problems when working with a NAT, stateful firewall.

# Raising server limits

A TCP connection utilizes a number of operating system resources. The OS kernel limits these available resources by imposing various upper bounds. In this section, we will raise the limits in order to increase the available resources for use.

## The queue size

The TCP stack tries to process data packets as soon as they arrive. If the rate of processing is low, the arriving data packets get queued up. The kernel usually specifies a limit on the total number of packets that can be queued at the server. The value is specified by the `net.core.netdev_max_backlog` key:

```
$ sysctl net.core.netdev_max_backlog
net.core.netdev_max_backlog = 300
```

Increase the queue size to a large value, such as `10000`:

```
$ sudo sysctl -w net.core.netdev_max_backlog=10000
net.core.netdev_max_backlog = 10000
```

## The listen socket queue size

The OS kernel defines a limit on the listen socket queue size. The limit is specified by the value of the `net.core.somaxconn` key:

```
$ sysctl net.core.somaxconn
net.core.somaxconn = 128
```

Now, increase the queue size to a large value, such as `2048`:

```
$ sudo sysctl -w net.core.somaxconn=2048
net.core.somaxconn = 2048
```

 It is important to note that the parameter will not make the intended impact. NGINX also limits the queue size of pending connections. The limit is defined by the backlog option of the listen directive in the NGINX configuration. By default, the variable defines a limit of -1 for the FreeBSD and OS X platforms and 511 for other platforms. Increase the values of backlog and `net.core.somaxconn` to alter the size of the pending connections queue.

# Half-opened connections

When the server accepts a connection, the connection waits for an acknowledgment from the client. Until that has happened, the connection is in a half-opened state. The OS kernel limits the total number of connections that can be in such a state. The server will drop new requests if the limits are exceeded. The limit is specified by the value of the `net.ipv4.tcp_max_syn_backlog` key:

```
$ sysctl net.ipv4.tcp_max_syn_backlog
net.ipv4.tcp_max_syn_backlog = 256
```

Increase the size to a large value, such as `2048`:

```
$ sysctl -w net.ipv4.tcp_max_syn_backlog = 2048
net.ipv4.tcp_max_syn_backlog = 2048
```

# Ephemeral ports

Ephemeral ports are the port numbers used by an operating system when an application opens a socket for communication. These ports are short-lived and are valid endpoints for the duration of the communication. The Linux kernel defines the ephemeral ports against the `net.ipv4.ip_local_port_range` key:

```
$ sysctl net.ipv4.ip_local_port_range
net.ipv4.ip_local_port_range = 32768    61000
```

The two values signify the minimum and maximum port values out of the total of 65,535 available ports on any system. These values may look adequately large, that is, 61000 - 32768 = 28232 is the number of available ports. It is important to note that 28,232 is the total number of available ports on the system. It does not turn out to be the number of concurrent connections that the server can serve.

As explained in the TCP states section, TCP will block sockets in the TIME_WAIT state with duration of MSL x 2. By default, the MSL is 60 seconds, which makes the TIME_WAIT period 120 seconds long. Thus, the server can only guarantee 28232/120 = 235 connections at any moment in time. If the server is acting as a proxy server, that is, it is serving content from upstream, then the number of connections will be half, that is, 235/2 = 117. Depending on your service and the load, this may not be a great number to look at!

> The number of ports guaranteed by the server at any moment in time can be increased by modifying the MSL. If the MSL is 30 seconds, the TIME_WAIT state comes out at 60 seconds. The result is 28232/60 = 470 available ports at any moment in time.

The range can be modified by specifying the minimum and maximum ports against the net.ipv4.ip_local_port_range key:

```
$ sudo sysctl -w net.ipv4.ip_local_port_range='15000 65000'
net.ipv4.ip_local_port_range = 15000 65000
```

This makes a total of 50,000 ports for TCP socket use.

# Open files

The kernel considers each opened socket as a file. It also imposes an upper bound on the total number of opened files. By default, the limit is set to 1,024 opened files:

```
$ ulimit -n
1024
```

Considering the total ephemeral socket range, this range is too low to serve the desired purpose. Under load, the limit may lead to socket failure with Too many opened files error messages in syslog.

The limits can be modified by changing the values in /etc/security/limits.conf. The file defines a soft limit and a hard limit against an item. Increase these values for the nofile item as an asterisk (*) with the user:

```
* soft nofile 50000
```

```
* hard nofile 50000
```

 The configuration specified previously alters the system-wide PAM limits. NGINX can also modify these limits using the worker_rlimit_nofile configuration directive covered in *Chapter 3, Tweaking NGINX Configuration*. It is preferable to modify the limits for NGINX rather than raise the overall system limits.

# Setting up the server

This chapter proposed changes to various kernel parameters. The changes were executed for each key using the sysctl command. The sysctl-w command was executed to write back changes made to the behavior until the next reboot. In order to make the change persistent across the machine reboot, the respective key-value pairs must be updated in the /etc/sysctl.conf file. The file can then be reloaded using the sysctl-p command to apply the configuration changes.

The following configuration sums up all the changes proposed in the chapter:

```
# TCP Stack changes
net.core.rmem_max = 16777216
net.ipv4.tcp_rmem = 4096 87380 16777216
net.core.wmem_max = 16777216
net.ipv4.tcp_wmem = 4096 16384 16777216
net.ipv4.tcp_fin_timeout = 20
net.ipv4.tcp_tw_reuse = 1
net.core.netdev_max_backlog = 10000
net.ipv4.ip_local_port_range = 15000 65000
net.core.somaxconn=2048
```

For the keys not mentioned in the preceding configuration, the kernels default values are good enough. If the kernel defaults do not match the proposed values, append the change to the preceding list. Reboot the machine to make sure that all changes to the configuration are picked up.

All the keys mentioned in this chapter are part of the Unix procfs under the /proc/sys directory. The /proc/sys directory contains directories representing the areas of the kernel, with each directory having files for the respective parameters. In order to know the value for a kernel parameter, for example, net.core.wmem_max, convert the key to a relative folder path under /proc/sys by replacing all dots (.) with slashes (/):

```
$ cat /proc/sys/net/core/wmem_max
16777216
```

Values can also be written to these files via the sudo command:

```
$ sudo bash -c 'echo 16777216 >
/proc/sys/net/core/wmem_max'
```

The modifications done in this manner are temporary, and sysctl should be used to permanently modify the values.

# Summary

This chapter was aimed at tweaking the network stack for performance-oriented communication. The chapter started with a discussion around TCP buffers and the bandwidth delay product (BDP). These buffers (send and receive) describe the TCP window size for socket connection. The window size governs the size of the TCP data packet. Traditionally, TCP-defined window sizes are of 16 bits. This can be increased to 32 bits, enabling transfer of larger data using the TCP scaling option.

This chapter described the TCP connection TIME_WAIT state. The TCP state is required to make sure that the socket handles all lingering packets before closing down. This is a necessary overhead as TIME_WAIT connections consume system ports and memory but do not serve any active clients. Since the state depends on the TCP maximum segment life (MSL), the MSL is reduced, enabling faster reuse of system resources.

Finally, the chapter listed ways to increase the TCP backlog, ephemeral ports, and available opened files. All of these are required to serve large numbers of concurrent clients.

Until now, we tweaked configurations to increase the utilization of the available resources. In the next chapter, we will try to remove slow data access using caching. The chapter will describe the caching alternatives available in NGINX and ways of using them.

# 6

# Using NGINX Cache

Slow data access can be improved drastically using a layer of caching. Caching temporarily saves recently used information in a store optimized for information lookup. This improves the server's performance by reducing the number of lookups required to load the same resource multiple times.

NGINX can cache static as well as dynamic content. If used in front of an upstream, NGINX will cache the responses received, thus doing away with future requests to the upstream server. In this chapter, we will cover the following topics:

- Caching static content
- Using FastCGI and the related cache
- Using Proxy and the related cache
- Using Memcache

## Caching static content

NGINX is already optimized to serve static content. In the case of high-traffic websites, the performance can be further improved using open_file_cache. The NGINX cache will store the recently used file descriptors and related metadata, such as modification time, size, and so on, in the cache. The cache will not store the contents of the requested file.

# open_file_cache

This directive enables a cache in NGINX that will store the following information:

- Opened file descriptors and related metadata, such as size, modification time, and so on
- The existence of files and directories
- Any errors related to lookup, such as "permission denied", "file not found", and so on

The cache defines a fixed size, and during overflows, it removes the **least recently used** (**LRU**) elements. The cache evicts elements after a period of inactivity. The directive is available under the http, server, and location sections of an NGINX configuration. The directive is disabled by default. Here's an example:

```
http{
open_file_cache max=1000 inactive=20s;
}
```

In the preceding configuration, a cache is defined for 1,000 elements. The inactive parameter configures the expiry time of 20 seconds. It is not necessary to set an inactive time period as the directive, by default, sets 60 seconds of inactivity period.

NGINX also defines a number of related directives that can be used to configure the behavior of open_file_cache during error and validity checks.

# open_file_cache_valid

NGINX's open_file_cache holds a snapshot of information. The snapshot may not be valid after a while as the information has changed at the source. The open_file_cache_valid directive defines the time period (in seconds), after which the elements in open_file_cache are revalidated. Here's an example:

```
http{
open_file_cache_valid 30s;
}
```

By default, the elements are validated after a period of 60 seconds. This directive can be configured under the http, server, and location sections of an NGINX configuration.

# open_file_cache_min_uses

NGINX will clear elements from the cache after the inactive time period. This directive can be used to configure the minimum number of accesses to mark the element as actively used. By default, the minimum number of accesses is set to 1 or more times. The directive can be configured under the `http`, `server`, and `location` sections of an NGINX configuration. Here's an example:

```
http{
open_file_cache_min_uses 4;
}
```

# open_file_cache_errors

As stated earlier, NGINX can cache errors that have occurred during file access. But this needs to be enabled by setting the `open_file_cache_errors` directive. If error caching is enabled, NGINX reports back the same error when the resource is accessed (without looking for resources). Here's an example:

```
http{
open_file_cache_errors on;
}
```

By default, the error cache is set to `off`. The directive can be configured under the `http`, `server`, and `location` sections of an NGINX configuration.

# Setting up the server

The following NGINX configuration summarizes the changes required to enable caching of static content:

```
http {
open_file_cache max=5000 inactive=20s;
open_file_cache_valid 60s;
open_file_cache_min_uses 5;
open_file_cache_errors off;

server {

# Rest configuration omitted for brevity
}
}
```

# Caching dynamic content

NGINX can cache responses from upstream servers. In this manner, it can significantly improve page load times and reduce the load on upstream servers. NGINX has various modules to perform upstream lookup, such as FastCGI, uwsgi, Proxy, and so on. Each upstream configuration presents its own set of directives to configure the related cache.

# Using FastCGI and the related cache

FastCGI is a language-independent protocol, which enables web servers to interface with various interactive programs. FastCGI is conceptually similar to **Common Gateway Interface (CGI)**. It is meant to be an open, secure, and fast web server interface to address performance issues of CGI, with improvements to reduce the associated overheads.

NGINX comes with the `ngx_http_fastcgi` module, which enables it to serve dynamic content from applications written in all kinds of languages, such as PHP, Python, Perl, and so on. Each of these languages has its own implementations for FastCGI, for example, PHP-FPM or any existing CGI implementation can be wrapped using the `fcgiwrap` utility to run on the FastCGI protocol.

In the remaining sections, we will configure NGINX to serve content using PHP via FCGI. Once the server is set up to use PHP, we will try to improve the performance using the corresponding FCGI cache.

## Installing PHP

In order to work with PHP scripts, we need to make sure that the `php` command is available on our box. While writing this book, PHP 5.6.14 is the latest stable version available on `http://php.net` and can be installed by performing the following steps:

Download and unpack the latest PHP archive:

```
$ wget -O php-5.6.8.tar.gz http://php.net/get/php-
5.6.8.tar.gz/from/this/mirror
$ tar -xvf php-5.6.8.tar.gz
```

The extracted archive contains the PHP source. The PHP binary can be configured by executing the `./configure` command in the extracted folder. The `configure` command gives loads of options to alter PHP defaults.

The PHP source bundles a FastCGI process manager, also known as PHP-FPM. This can be enabled by passing the `--enable-fpm` option to the `configure` command:

```
$ cd php-5.6.8
$ ./configure --enable-fpm -q
+---------------------------------------------------------------------+
| License: |
| This software is subject to the PHP License, available in this |
| distribution in the file LICENSE. By continuing this installation |
| process, you are bound by the terms of this license agreement. |
| If you do not agree with the terms of this license, you must abort |
| the installation process at this point. |
+---------------------------------------------------------------------+


Thank you for using PHP.
```

 The PHP source requires the `libxml` and `libevent` development libraries. Make sure that the `libxml2-dev` and `libevent-dev` packages are installed:

```
$ sudo apt-get install libxml2-dev libevent-dev
```

Post configuration, run the `make` command to generate the PHP binary:

```
$ make --quiet
```

Next, execute the `make` command with the `install` option to install php and related packages on the system path:

```
$ sudo make install
Installing PHP CLI binary:        /usr/local/bin/
Installing PHP CLI man page:      /usr/local/php/man/man1/
Installing PHP FPM binary:        /usr/local/sbin/
Installing PHP FPM config:        /usr/local/etc/
Installing PHP FPM man page:      /usr/local/php/man/man8/
Installing PHP FPM status page:   /usr/local/php/php/fpm/
Installing PHP CGI binary:        /usr/local/bin/
Installing PHP CGI man page:      /usr/local/php/man/man1/
```

Verify the PHP installation by running the `php` and `php-fpm` commands with the `-v` option:

```
$ php -v
PHP 5.6.8 (cli) (built: Apr 27 2015 10:11:53)
Copyright (c) 1997-2015 The PHP Group
Zend Engine v2.6.0, Copyright (c) 1998-2015 Zend Technologies

$ php-fpm -v
PHP 5.6.8 (fpm-fcgi) (built: Apr 27 2015 10:12:03)
Copyright (c) 1997-2015 The PHP Group
Zend Engine v2.6.0, Copyright (c) 1998-2015 Zend Technologies
```

> We could also install PHP from the Ubuntu repositories using the `apt-get` command. Unlike the `configure` command, which generates the `fpm` package, we need to install the `php5-fpm` package to get PHP FastCGI support. The only caveat here is that the PHP version will not be the latest one. The following command shows this:
>
> `$ sudo apt-get install php5php5-fpm`

## Deploying PHP scripts

We are done with installing the `php` and `php-fpm` packages on our box. Next, we want to use these to run PHP scripts. We have built the following PHP script to show dates. All PHP code is written within the `<?php ?>` block. I will provide an explanation of the code; however, please refer to the PHP tutorials for a complete overview of the language. The following commands show this:

```
<!DOCTYPE html>
<html lang="en">
<head>
<title>Check dates</title>
<link href="css/bootstrap.min.css" rel="stylesheet">
</head>
<body>
<?phpdate_default_timezone_set('GMT'); ?>
<div class="container">
<div class="jumbotron">
<h1>Checking dates</h1>
</div>
<div class="row">
```

```
<h4>Today is <?php echo '<mark>' . date('l'). '</mark>, '.
date('d-M'). ' and current time is ' .
date('h:i:sa');?></h4></div>
<div class="row">
<h4> Tomorrow will be
<?php $d=strtotime('tomorrow'); echo date('l', $d) .', '.date('d-
M', $d) . '.';?></h4></div>
<div class="row">
<h4> Next Sunday is on
<?php $d=strtotime('next Sunday');echo date('d-M', $d)
.'.';?></h4></div>
</div>
</body>
</html>
```

The first PHP statement (line 8) sets the default time zone to GMT using the `date_default_timezone_set` function:

- Next, we print today's information using the `date` function (line 14) to determine current day (l), date (d-m), and time (h:i:sa)

- The dot (.) is used as an operator (line 14) to concatenate different strings into one

- Similarly, we print tomorrow's information using the `strtotime` and `date` functions (line 17) to determine the day (l) and date (d-m)

- At last, we determine the next Sunday's information using the `strtotime` and `date` functions (line 20)

We can pack the script as a `date.php` parallel to `index.html` in our "Hello, world!" example. This will allow us to use some basic styling as well:

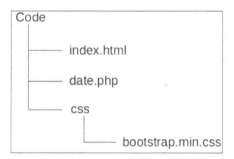

# Configuring php-fpm

Now, we need to run the PHP-FPM server and configure the connector in NGINX. The server also requires a configuration file, specifying server settings, such as `port`, `user`, `connection`, `pool` and so on, and reports errors if the configuration file is not found:

```
$ sudo php-fpm
ERROR: failed to open configuration file '/usr/local/etc/php-fpm.conf':
No such file or directory (2)
ERROR: FPM initialization failed
```

The PHP installation provides a default file that can be used to start the FPM server. The file can be in the `/usr/local/etc/php-fpm.conf.default` location, or as specified in the installation output message. Copy the default file to the error path specified in the server output. Modify the process user and group names to `www-data` by doing a lookup for user and group directives in the file:

```
; Unix user/group of processes
; Note: The user is mandatory. If the group is not set, the default
user's group
; will be used.
user = www-data
group = www-data
```

The default the server will run on port `9000`. Modify it to run on a Unix socket by specifying a Unix socket address in the `listen` directive:

```
; 'ip.add.re.ss:port' - to listen on a TCP socket to a
; specific IPv4 address on a specific port;
; 'port' - to listen on a TCP socket to all
; IPv4 addresses on a specific port;
; '/path/to/unix/socket' - to listen on a unix socket.
listen = /var/run/php-fpm.sock
```

Since we have configured the `unix` socket, we also need to set the socket owner and group. Specify the owner and group names in the `listen.owner` and `listen.group` directives respectively:

```
; Set permissions for unix socket, if one is used. In Linux,
; read/write permissions must be set in order to allow
; connections from a web server.
listen.owner = www-data
```

```
listen.group = www-data
listen.mode = 0660
```

We have now configured the PHP-FPM server correctly, and it should start listening at the address specified. Restart the server using the `php-fpm` command, as shown here:

```
$ sudo php-fpm
```

# Configuring NGINX FastCGI

Until now, we have written some PHP code and have configured a PHP server to render the content. But NGINX is still not configured to interpret PHP. If we try to access the `/hello/date.php` location, the browser will download the file rather than displaying the contents. Configure FastCGI in NGINX using the following directives. In addition to the directives, NGINX creates the `$fastcgi_script_name` variable, which is set using the request URI.

## fastcgi_pass

This directive is used to specify the address of the FastCGI server. The address can be in any of the following forms:

- It can be a domain name or IP address along with the port, that is, `location:port`
- It can be a `unix` socket address specified with the `unix:` prefix, for example, `unix:/var/run/php-fpm.sock`
- It can be a group of servers created using the NGINX upstream directive

This directive is only available under the `location` and `if` and in `location` sections of an NGINX configuration. Here's an example:

```
location ~ \.php($|/){
fastcgi_passunix:/var/run/php-fpm.sock;
}
```

## fastcgi_param

This directive allows the configuration of request parameters passed to the FastCGI server. The directive allows a parameter to be declared as a `name-value` pair. It is available under the `http`, `server`, and `location` sections of an NGINX configuration. Here's an example:

```
http{
fastcgi_param REDIRECT_STATUS 200;
}
```

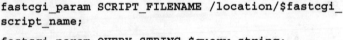

Each FastCGI server has its own set of parameters. The PHP implementation makes it mandatory to pass the SCRIPT_FILENAME and QUERY_STRING parameters. The filename must specify the script to execute, and QUERY_STRING is required to pass request parameters:

```
fastcgi_param SCRIPT_FILENAME /location/$fastcgi_
script_name;

fastcgi_param QUERY_STRING $query_string;
```

If there are any POST requests by PHP, then in addition to the preceding parameters, the following three parameters are also required:

```
fastcgi_param REQUEST_METHOD $request_method;
fastcgi_param CONTENT_TYPE $content_type;
fastcgi_param CONTENT_LENGTH $content_length;
```

## fastcgi_index

This directive is used to specify the index script that should be executed if the URL ends in a slash (/) and does not specify a script to execute. The directive sets the value in the $fastcgi_script_name variable. This directive is available under the http, server, and location sections of an NGINX configuration. Here's an example:

```
http{
fastcgi_index index.php;
}
```

## fastcgi_split_path_info

This directive specifies a regular expression that can be used to capture and update the $fastcgi_script_name variable from the request URL. In addition to the $fastcgi_script_name variable, the directive also specifies the $fastcgi_path_info variable, which is also captured by the regular expression. This directive is available under the location section of an NGINX configuration. Here's an example:

```
http{
fastcgi_split_path_info ^(.+\.php)(.*)$;
}
```

The expression must capture two arguments: the first one for $fastcgi_script_name and the second one for $fastcgi_path_info.

# fastcgi_bind

This directive can be used to specify and address FastCGI communication. By default, the directive is set to `off`. NGINX therefore auto assigns the local IP address for communication. This directive is available under the `http`, `server`, and `location` sections of an NGINX configuration.

# fastcgi_ignore_headers

This directive enables NGINX to ignore processing of certain FastCGI response headers, namely, `X-Accel-Expires`, `Expires`, `Cache-Control`, `Set-Cookie`, `Vary`, `X-Accel-Redirect`, `X-Accel-Charset`, `X-Accel-Buffering`, and `X-Accel-Limit-Rate`. If not disabled, the fields cause the following behavior:

- The caching is controlled by the `X-Accel-Expires`, `Expires`, `Cache-Control`, `Set-Cookie`, and `Vary` header fields
- An internal redirect is performed using `X-Accel-Redirect`
- The response character set is controlled by `X-Accel-Charset`
- The buffering of responses is controlled by `X-Accel-Buffering`
- The rate of response transmission to the client is controlled by `X-Accel-Limit-Rate`

This directive is available under the `http`, `server`, and `location` sections of an NGINX configuration.

# fastcgi_pass_request_headers / fastcgi_pass_request_body

This directive indicates whether the request header and body should be passed to the FastCGI server or not. By default, both the directives are set to `on`. Both these directives are available under `http`, `server`, and `location` sections of NGINX configuration. Here's an example:

```
http{
fastcgi_pass_request_headers on;
fastcgi_pass_request_body on;
}
```

# fastcgi_connect_timeout / fastcgi_send_timeout / fastcgi_read_timeout

The `fastcgi_connect_timeout` directive sets the timeout to establish a connection between NGINX and the FastCGI server.

The `fastcgi_send_timeout` directive sets the timeout to write a request to the FastCGI server. The `fastcgi_read_timeout` directive sets the timeout to read a response from the FastCGI server.

All the three directives have the default value of 60 seconds and are available under the `http`, `server`, and `location` sections of an NGINX configuration. Here's an example:

```
http{
fastcgi_send_timeout 30s
fastcgi_connect_timeout 30s
fastcgi_read_timeout 30s
}
```

It is important to note that the connection will be closed if the timeout specifies any `fastcgi_send_timeout` directive and the `fastcgi_read_timeout` directive expires.

## fastcgi_store / fastcgi_store_access

The `fastcgi_store` directive enables the saving of responses from upstream to the disk as files. By default, the directive is set to `off`. The directive can be turned on, which will save the response in the directive's root location. The directive can also specify a path, using variables, which is used to determine the file's location. The directive is available under the `http`, `server`, and `location` sections of an NGINX configuration. Here's an example:

```
location /php{
fastcgi_store on;
fastcgi_store_access user:rw group:rw all:r;
root /location;
}
```

The `$fastcgi_store_access` directive can be used to specify the permissions for the created files.

## Setting up the server

The previous section covered the FastCGI directives available in NGINX. Now, let's try to configure the communication between NGINX and the PHP-FPM server.

Add a location directive to handle `.php` files and configure NGINX FastCGI upstream in the following manner:

```
location ~* /hello/(.+\.php)$ {
fastcgi_pass unix:/var/run/php-fpm.sock;
fastcgi_param SCRIPT_FILENAME /code-location/$1;
```

```
fastcgi_param QUERY_STRING $query_string;
fastcgi_param REQUEST_METHOD $request_method;
fastcgi_param CONTENT_TYPE $content_type;
fastcgi_param CONTENT_LENGTH $content_length;
}
```

The preceding configuration does the following:

- The location directive does case-insensitive regular expression (`~* /hello/ (.+\.php)$`) matching to server URLs such as `/hello/date.php`

- The location regular expression captures the `$1` argument, which is then used in the `fastcgi_param` argument to specify the script location

- `fastcgi_pass` specifies the `unix` socket on which the FPM server is listening

Now, access the location `http://server/date.php`; it should generate an HTML, as shown in the following screenshot:

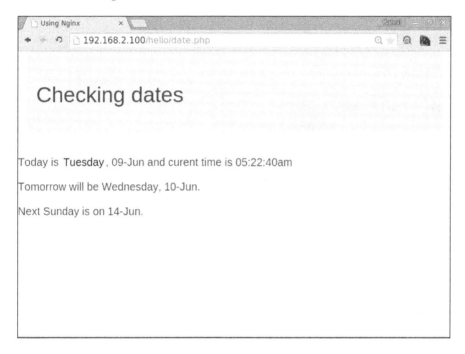

# Configuring the FastCGI cache

We have successfully set up a connection between NGINX and PHP. Now, we want to cache the content served from PHP. NGINX provides the following directives to configure the FastCGI cache.

# fastcgi_cache_path

This directive is used to define a FastCGI cache. The directive has a couple of arguments that can be used to configure the cache behavior. It is mandatory to specify the disk location, cache name, and cache size. The cache also has an inactive time period, that is, the time after which data will be purged from the cache. The `levels` parameter can be used to define the hierarchy while writing data to the cache. The directive is only available under the `http` section of an NGINX configuration. Here's an example:

```
http{
fastcgi_cache_path /var/cache/NGINX keys_zone=mycache:10m
inactive=15m;
}
```

By default, the inactive period is set to `10` minutes. NGINX also runs a cache manager, which will remove the oldest entry once the cache reaches its maximum size as defined by the optional `max_size` parameter.

Cache loading is accomplished by a cache loader process. The `option` parameter specified by the directives, namely `loader_files`, `loader_sleep`, and `loader_threshold`, can alter the cache loading behavior.

# fastcgi_cache_key

This directive defines the key for cache lookup. The directive is available under the `http`, `server`, and `location` sections of an NGINX configuration. Here's an example:

```
http{
fastcgi_cache_key "$request_method$request_uri";
}
```

# fastcgi_cache

This directive enables the use of a previously defined memory cache using the `fastcgicache_path` directive. The `fastcgi_cache` directive identifies the memory zone by the name specified in the configuration. By default, the cache is set to `off`. The directive is available under the `http`, `server`, and `location` sections of an NGINX configuration. Here's an example:

```
http{
fastcgi_cache mycache;
}
```

# fastcgi_cache_valid

This directive enables NGINX to define the cache time period depending on the HTTP response code. If the HTTP response code is not specified, then only the `200`, `301`, and `302` response codes are cached. The directive also specifies any parameter that can be used to cache all response code files. The directive is available under the `http`, `server`, and `location` sections of an NGINX configuration. Here's an example:

```
http{
fastcgi_cache_valid 200 302 10m;
fastcgi_cache_valid any 1m;
}
```

Cache control fields in the response header have higher precedence than the directive. The processing of the response header can be turned off using the `fastcgi_ignore_headers` directive.

# fastcgi_no_cache

This directive defines the conditions under which the response will not be saved to the cache. The directive takes a list of the parameters that are evaluated at runtime. If any of them are nonempty and nonzero, the response will not be cached. The directive is available under the `http`, `server`, and `location` sections of an NGINX configuration. Here's an example:

```
http{
fastcgi_no_cache $http_pragma $cookie_nocache;
}
```

The preceding configuration will not cache the response if the header contains the Pragma field or if a no-cache cookie has been set.

# fastcgi_cache_bypass

This directive defines the conditions under which NGINX will not perform cache lookup. The directive takes a list of parameters that are evaluated at runtime. If any of them is nonempty and nonzero, the response will not be cached. The directive is available under the `http`, `server`, and `location` sections of an NGINX configuration:

```
http{
fastcgi_bypass_cache $http_pragma $cookie_nocache;
}
```

The preceding configuration will not perform a lookup on the cache if the header contains the Pragma field or if a no-cache cookie has been set.

## fastcgi_cache_methods

This directive defines the list of HTTP methods that will be cached. By default, the GET and HEAD methods are cached. The directive is available under the http, server, and location sections of an NGINX configuration. Here's an example:

```
http{
fastcgi_cache_methods GET HEAD;
}
```

## fastcgi_cache_use_stale

This directive defines the error conditions under which a stale response can be used from the cache. The directive defines all error conditions served by NGINX as parameters. By default, the directive is set to off. This directive is available under the http, server, and location sections of an NGINX configuration. Here's an example:

```
http{
fastcgi_cache_use_stale http_500 http_503;
}
```

## Setting up the server

The following configuration adds support for FastCGI cache in NGINX and enables it for the deployed PHP scripts:

```
http{
fastcgi_cache_path /etc/NGINX/cache keys_zone=phpCache:100m
inactive=60m;
fastcgi_cache_key "$request_method$host$request_uri";
server{
location ~* /hello/(.+\.php)$ {
fastcgi_passunix:/var/run/php-fpm.sock;
fastcgi_param SCRIPT_FILENAME /code-location/$1;
fastcgi_param QUERY_STRING $query_string;
fastcgi_param REQUEST_METHOD $request_method;
fastcgi_param CONTENT_TYPE $content_type;
fastcgi_param CONTENT_LENGTH $content_length;
fastcgi_cache phpCache;
fastcgi_cache_valid 1m;
add_header X-FastCGI-Cache $upstream_cache_status;
}
# Rest NGINX configuration omitted for brevity
}
}
```

The preceding configuration does the following things:

- The `fastcgi_cache_path` directive creates a cache for the specified size
- The `fastcgi_cache_key` directive defines the key format for cache lookup
- The `fastcgi_cache` directive in the location section enables the cache for all requests served by the block
- The `fastcgi_cache_valid` will cache a successful response for 1 minute
- Additionally, the server adds the `X-FastCGI-Cache` field in the response header, indicating the status of the cache hit

Since we have added a field in the header, it can be used to validate whether the request has been served from the cache. Here's an example:

```
$ curl -I http://192.168.2.100/hello/date.php
HTTP/1.1 200 OK
Server: NGINX/1.7.12 (Ubuntu)
Date: Thu, 30 Apr 2015 08:50:30 GMT
Content-Type: text/html; charset=UTF-8
Connection: keep-alive
X-Powered-By: PHP/5.6.8
X-FastCGI-Cache: MISS


$ curl -I http://192.168.2.100/hello/date.php
.. .. .. ..
X-FastCGI-Cache: HIT
```

# Using Proxy and the related cache

NGINX can be used to Proxy an existing HTTP server. There can be many reasons to do this. We may want to use NGINX in front of Tomcat or Jetty. If there are multiple applications running at different locations, then NGINX can take care of the routing requests, depending on the request URL. NGINX can be used with Apache by configuring the Proxy module.

In the remaining sections, we will configure NGINX to serve content using Python-Flask. Once the server is set up, we will try to improve the performance using the corresponding Proxy cache.

# Installing Python and Flask

In order to work with Python, we need to make sure that the Python command is available on our box. It can be downloaded from http://www.python.org/. At the time of writing this, Python 3.4.3 is the latest stable version available. It can be installed by performing the following steps:

1. Download and unpack the latest Python archive:

```
$ wget https://www.python.org/ftp/python/3.4.3/
Python-3.4.3.tgz

$ tar -xvf Python-3.4.3.tgz
```

2. The extracted archive contains the Python source code. We can configure Python by executing the ./configure command in the extracted folder:

```
$ ./configure

configure: creating ./config.status

config.status: creating Makefile.pre

config.status: creating Modules/Setup.config

config.status: creating Misc/python.pc

config.status: creating Misc/python-config.sh

config.status: creating Modules/ld_so_aix

config.status: creating pyconfig.h

creating Modules/Setup

creating Modules/Setup.local

creating Makefile
```

>  Python 3.4 and above include Python Package Manager, namely the pip command. The pip command requires the openssl and libssl-dev libraries. Make sure that they are available:
>
> ```
> $ sudo apt-get install libssl-dev openssl
> ```

3. After configuration, run the make command to generate the Python binary:

```
$ make --quiet
```

4. Next, execute the make command with the install option to install Python and its related packages on your system path:

```
$ sudo make install
```

5. Verify the Python installation by running the `python3` command with the `-V` option:

```
$ python3 -V
Python 3.4.3
```

6. Now, we need to set up Flask, a web framework available in Python. Install it using the `pip` command:

```
$ sudo python3 -m pip install flask
```

# Building a Python application

In the previous section, we prepared our box for Python development. In this section, we will build an application that will show certain dates, as done in the PHP application discussed earlier in the chapter. The section will provide an explanation of the application code. However, please refer to the Python documentation for a complete overview of the language.

The application consists of an HTML template, namely `date.html`, which is used to render the content:

```
<!DOCTYPE html>
<html lang="en">
<head>
<title>Checking Dates</title>
<link href="css/bootstrap.min.css" rel="stylesheet">
</head>
<body>
<div class="container">
<div class="jumbotron">
<h1>Checking dates</h1>
</div>
<div class="row">
<h4>Today is <mark>{{ today.day }}</mark>,{{ today.date }} and
current time is {{ today.time }}</h4></div>
<div class="row">
<h4> Tomorrow will be {{ tomorrow.day}}, {{ tomorrow.date
}}.</h4></div>
<div class="row">
<h4> Next {{ nextday.day }} is on {{ nextday.date }}</h4></div>
</div>
</body>
</html>
```

The template contains standard HTML syntax. The parts of text that are meant to be replaced by Python variables are enclosed within {{ }}.

The application also packs a Python script, namely date.py, which is used to compute the variables and render the content:

```
from flask import Flask
from flask import render_template
import datetime

class AppdateTime :
def __init__(self, day, date, time):
self.day = day
self.date = date
self.time = time

@app.route("/")
defcomputeDate():
d = datetime.datetime.now();
today = AppdateTime(d.strftime("%A"),d.strftime("%d %B"),
d.strftime("%H:%M:%S %p"))
d = d + datetime.timedelta(days=1)
tom = AppdateTime(d.strftime("%A"),d.strftime("%d %B"),
d.strftime("%H:%M:%S %p"))
d = d + datetime.timedelta(days=6)
nxt = AppdateTime(d.strftime("%A"),d.strftime("%d %B"),
d.strftime("%H:%M:%S %p"))
return render_template('date.html',today=today, tomorrow=tom,
nextday=nxt)
app = Flask(__name__)
if __name__ == "__main__":
app.run()
```

The preceding script does the following things:

- The couple of lines at the top import the Flask framework and its related tools
- Next, we define an Appdatetime class that can be used to find the day, date, and time
- The computeDate method computes the dates and then fills date.html to send back the complete HTML
- The script uses the datetime and strftime Python methods to calculate dates
- The computeDate method is mapped to the / path using the app.route annotation
- Finally, we run the Flask engine and bind it to the localhost address.

Pack date.html in a folder named templates that are parallel to the date.py location. The application will have the following structure:

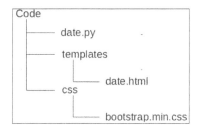

Now, run the Flask server using the python3 command:

```
$ python3 date.py
* Running on http://127.0.0.1:5000/ (Press CTRL+C to quit)
```

The web page should be up on the 5000 port of the server. It is important to note that we have packed a CSS that is not being served now. In the next section, we will try to configure static resources from NGINX, while serving the dynamic content from the Flask server. Here's the web page:

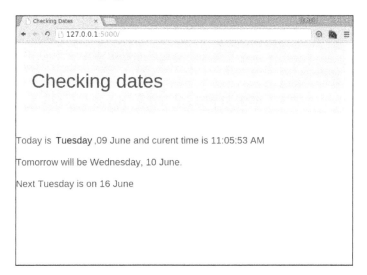

# Configuring NGINX Proxy

In the preceding section, we developed a Python application running on the 5000 port. Now, we want to configure NGINX to Proxy the server using the following directives. We will also try to cache the response from the Python server by enabling the proxy cache.

In addition to the directives, the NGINX Proxy module also creates the `$proxy_host`, `$proxy_port`, and `$proxy_add_x_forward_for` variables that can be used at various places such as Proxy headers.

## proxy_pass

This directive can be used to specify the protocol, address, and URL (optional) of the upstream server. The protocol takes the value `http` or `https`. The address can be in any of the following forms:

- It can be a domain name or IP address along with the port, that is, `location:port`
- It can be a `unix` socket address specified with a `unix:` prefix and enclosed within colons, for example, `unix:/var/run/server.sock:`
- It can be a group of servers created using the NGINX upstream directive

This directive is only available under the `location and if` and in `location` sections of an NGINX configuration. Here's an example:

```
location /myloc/{
proxy_pass http://unix:/var/run/server.sock:/loc;
}
```

## proxy_method

This directive sets the HTTP method passed to the proxy server instead of the version specified by the client. The directive is available under the `http`, `server`, and `location` sections of an NGINX configuration.

## proxy_set_header

This directive is used to define header fields passed in the upstream request. The fields can have values in the form of variables and text. If there is a field with an empty string (`""`) as its value, it will not be passed in the upstream request. The directive is available under the `http`, `server`, and `location` sections of an NGINX configuration. Here's an example:

```
location /myloc/{
proxy_set_header Host $proxy_host;
proxy_set_header Accept-Charset UTF-8;
}
```

By default, NGINX sets only two fields, namely `Host` with the `$proxy_host` value and `connection` with the `close` value.

## proxy_http_version

This directive sets the version of HTTP for requests to the upstream server. By default, the value is 1.0. Version 1.1 should be used for `keepalive` connections. The directive is available under the `http`, `server`, and `location` sections of an NGINX configuration.

> In order to work with upstream `keepalive` connections, the connection header needs to be set. NGINX, by default, sets the header field to close. Use `proxy_set_header` to set the `keepalive` value in the connection header. Here's an example:
>
> ```
> location /myloc/{
>         proxy_set_header Connection keep-alive;
>         proxy_http_version 1.1
> }
> ```

## proxy_pass_request_headers / proxy_pass_request_body

These directives indicate whether the request header and body should be passed to the upstream server or not. By default, both the directives are set to `on`. The directives are available under the `http`, `server`, and `location` sections of an NGINX configuration. Here's an example:

```
http{
proxy_pass_request_headers on;
proxy_pass_request_body on;
}
```

## proxy_ignore_headers

This directive enables NGINX to ignore the processing of certain upstream response headers, namely `X-Accel-Expires`, `Expires`, `Cache-Control`, `Set-Cookie`, `Vary`, `X-Accel-Redirect`, `X-Accel-Charset`, `X-Accel-Buffering`, and `X-Accel-Limit-Rate`. If not disabled, the fields cause the following behavior:

- The caching is controlled by `X-Accel-Expires`, `Expires`, `Cache-Control`, `Set_Cookie`, and `Vary` header fields

- An internal redirect is performed using X-Accel-Redirect
- The response character set is controlled by X-Accel-Charset
- The buffering of responses is controlled by X-Accel-Buffering
- The rate of response transmission to the client is controlled by X-Accel-Limit-Rate

This directive is available under the http, server, and location sections of an NGINX configuration.

# proxy_connect_timeout / proxy_send_timeout / proxy_read_timeout

The proxy_connect_timeout directive sets the timeout to establish a connection between NGINX and the Proxy server.

The proxy_send_timeout directive sets the timeout to write a request to the Proxy server. The proxy_read_timeout directive sets the timeout to read a response from the Proxy server.

All the directives have a default value of 60 seconds and are available under the http, server, and location sections of an NGINX configuration. Here's an example:

```
http{
proxy_send_timeout 30s;
proxy_connect_timeout 30s;
proxy_read_timeout 30s;
}
```

It is important to note that the connection will be closed if the timeout specifies any proxy_send_timeout directives and proxy_read_timeoutdirective expires.

# proxy_store / proxy_store_access

The proxy_store directive enables saving responses from upstream to the disk as files. By default, the directive is off. The directive can be turned on, which will save the response in the directive's root location. The directive can also specify a path, using variables, which is used to determine the file's location. The directive is available under the http, server, and location sections of an NGINX configuration:

```
location /myloc{
proxy_store on;
proxy_store_access user:rw group:rw all:r;
```

```
root /location;
}
```

The `proxy_store_access` directive can be used to specify the permissions for the created files. By default, the directive grants read-write permissions to the file owner only. This directive is available under the `http`, `server`, and `location` sections of an NGINX configuration.

# proxy_cache_path

This directive is used to define a cache. The directive has a couple of arguments that can be used to configure the cache behavior. It is mandatory to specify the disk location, cache name, and cache size. The cache also has an `inactive` time period, that is, the time after which data will be purged from the cache. The `levels` parameter can be used to define the hierarchy while writing data to the cache. The directive is only available under the `http` section of an NGINX configuration. Here's an example:

```
http{
proxy_cache_path /var/cache/NGINX keys_zone=mycache:10m
inactive=15m;
}
```

By default, the `inactive` period is set to `10` minutes. NGINX also runs a cache manager, which will remove the oldest entry once the cache reaches its maximum size as defined by the optional `max_size` parameter.

Cache loading is accomplished by a cache loader process. The option parameter specified by the directive, namely, `loader_files`, `loader_sleep`, and `loader_threshold` can alter the cache loading behavior.

# proxy_cache_key

This directive defines the key for cache lookup. The directive is available under the `http`, `server`, and `location` sections of an NGINX configuration. Here's an example:

```
http{
proxy_cache_key "$request_method$request_uri";
}
```

# proxy_cache

This directive enables the use of a previously defined memory cache using the proxy cache_path directive. The `proxy_cache` directive identifies the memory zone by the name specified in the configuration. By default, the cache is set to `off`. The directive is available under the `http`, `server`, and `location` sections of an NGINX configuration. Here's an example:

```
http{
proxy_cache mycache;
}
```

# proxy_cache_valid

This directive enables NGINX to define the cache time period depending on the HTTP response code. If the HTTP response code is not specified, then only the `200`, `301`, and `302` response codes are cached. The directive also specifies any parameter that can be used to cache all response code files. The directive is available under the `http`, `server`, and `location` sections of an NGINX configuration. Here's an example:

```
http{
proxy_cache_valid 200 302 10m;
proxy_cache_valid any 1m;
}
```

Cache control fields in the response header have a higher precedence than the directive. The processing of the response header can be turned `off` using the `proxy_ignore_headers` directive.

# proxy_no_cache

This directive defines the conditions under which the response will not be saved to the cache. The directive takes a list of parameters that are evaluated at runtime. If any of them is nonempty and nonzero, the response will not be cached. The directive is available under the `http`, `server`, and `location` sections of an NGINX configuration. Here's an example:

```
http{
proxy_no_cache $http_pragma $cookie_nocache;
}
```

The preceding configuration will not cache the response if the header contains the Pragma field, or if a `no-cache` cookie has been set.

# proxy_cache_bypass

This directive defines the conditions in which NGINX will not perform cache lookup. The directive takes a list of parameters that are evaluated at runtime. If either of them is nonempty and nonzero, the response will not be cached. The directive is available under the `http`, `server`, and `location` sections of an NGINX configuration. Here's an example:

```
http{
proxy_bypass_cache $http_pragma $cookie_nocache;
}
```

The preceding configuration will not perform cache lookup if the header contains the Pragma field, or if a no-cache cookie has been set.

# proxy_cache_methods

This directive defines the list of HTTP methods that will be cached. By default, the GET and HEAD methods are cached. The directive is available under the `http`, `server`, and `location` sections of an NGINX configuration. Here's an example:

```
http{
proxy_cache_methods GET HEAD;
}
```

# proxy_cache_use_stale

This directive defines the error conditions under which a stale response can be used from the cache. The directive defines all error conditions served by NGINX as parameters. By default, the directive is set to `off`. This directive is available under the `http`, `server`, and `location` sections of an NGINX configuration. Here's an example:

```
http{
proxy_cache_use_stale http_500 http_503;
}
```

# Setting up the server

The following configuration enables NGINX to serve content from the Flask application. NGINX is also configured to serve the CSS file, which is a part of the Python application. The cache directives are used to enable the support of the Proxy cache for the Python application. Here's how NGINX is configured for Flash:

```
http{
proxy_cache_path /etc/NGINX/pythoncachekeys_zone=pythonCache:100m
inactive=60m;
proxy_cache_key "$request_method$host$request_uri";
server{
location /python/css/ {
alias "/code-path/css/";
}

location /python/ {
proxy_pass http://127.0.0.1:5000/;
proxy_cache pythonCache;
proxy_cache_valid any 1m;
add_header X-Proxy-Cache $upstream_cache_status;
}
# Rest NGINX configuration omitted for brevity
}
}
```

The preceding configuration does the following things:

- The `proxy_cache_path` directive creates a cache for the specified size
- The `proxy_cache_key` directive defines the key format for cache lookup
- The location directive for `/python/css` enables NGINX to serve all static content
- The location directive for `/python/` forwards all requests to the server running at `127.0.0.1:5000`
- The `proxy_cache` directive in the location section enables the cache for all requests served by the block
- The `proxy_cache_valid` directive caches a successful response for 1 minute

Additionally, the server adds the `X-Proxy-Cache` field in the response header, indicating the status of a cache hit.

Now, access the location `http://server/python/`. A screenshot similar to the following one will be displayed:

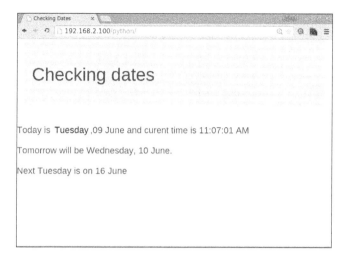

Since we have added a field in the header, it can be used to validate whether the request has been served from the cache:

```
$ curl -I http://192.168.2.100/python/
HTTP/1.1 200 OK
Server: NGINX/1.7.12 (Ubuntu)
Date: Thu, 30 Apr 2015 08:50:30 GMT
Content-Type: text/html; charset=UTF-8
Connection: keep-alive
X-Proxy-Cache: MISS

$ curl -I http://192.168.2.100/python/
.. .. .. ..
X-Proxy-Cache: HIT
```

# Using Memcache

Memcache is a generic-purpose memory-caching system. It is often used to speed up slow data access. The NGINX memcached module presents various directives that can be configured to serve content directly from Memcache, thus avoiding requests to the upstream server.

In addition to the directives, the module also creates the $memcached_key variable, which is used to perform cache lookup. Before using the Memcache lookup, a value must be set in the $memcached_key variable, which is determined from the request URL.

 It is important to note that the NGINX Memcache module only performs the lookup for the specified $memcached_key variable. It does not perform any write backs to the cache for the specified key. A value corresponding to the key should be in the cache beforehand, written by means external to NGINX.

## memcached_pass

This directive is used to specify the location of the memcached server. The address can be specified in any of the following ways:

- A domain name or IP address, along with an optional port
- A Unix domain socket specified with the unix: prefix
- A group of servers created using the NGINX upstream directive

The directive is only available under the location and if and in location sections of an NGINX configuration. Here's an example:

```
location /myloc/{
set $memached_key $uri;
memcached_pass localhost:11211;
}
```

## memcached_connect_timeout / memcached_send_timeout / memcached_read_timeout

The memcached_connect_timeout directive sets the timeout to establish a connection between NGINX and the memcached server.

The memcached_send_timeout directive sets the timeout to write a request to the memcached server. The memcached_read_timeout directive sets the timeout for reading a response from the memcached server.

All the directives have a default value of 60 seconds and are available under the `http`, `server`, and `location` sections of an NGINX configuration. Here's an example:

```
http{
memcached_send_timeout 30s;
memcached_connect_timeout 30s;
memcached_read_timeout 30s;
}
```

It is important to note that the connection will be closed if the timeout specifies any `memcached_send_timeout` directive, and `memcached_read_timeout` directive expires.

# memcached_bind

This directive can be used to specify and address in order to communicate with the memcached server. By default, the directive is set to `off`. Thus, NGINX auto-assigns the local IP address for communication. The directive is available under the `http`, `server`, and `location` sections of an NGINX configuration.

# Setting up the server

In this section, we will configure NGINX to serve requests from the memcached server for the Python application that was developed earlier in the chapter. When NGINX is unable to find the key in the memcached server, it forwards the request to the Python application. The application then serves the request and puts the responses in the memcached server for future requests. Here's how we configure NGINX for Memcache:

```
server{
location /python/css/ {
alias "/code/location/css/";
}

location /python/ {
set $memcached_key "$request_method$request_uri";
charset utf-8;
memcached_pass 127.0.0.1:11211;
error_page 404 502 504 = @pythonfallback;
default_type text/html;
}

location @pythonfallback {
rewrite ^/python/(.*) /$1 break;
```

```
proxy_pass http://127.0.0.1:5000;
proxy_set_header X-Cache-Key "$request_method$request_uri";
}
# Rest NGINX configuration omitted for brevity


}
```

The preceding NGINX configuration does the following things:

- Setting $memcached_key for cache lookup
- Specifying the address of the memcached server using the memcached_pass directive
- Using a fallback to serve content from Python server upstream for errors such as 404
- Additionally requesting the Python server upstream, thus setting a header field for the lookup key

 In order to interact with the memcached server from Python, we would require the python3-memcached package. Install it using the pip command:

```
$ sudopython3 -m pip install python3-memcached
```

```
from flask import Flask
from flask import render_template
from flask import request
import memcache
zsq23
cache = memcache.Client(["127.0.0.1:11211"])

@app.after_request
defprocessResponse(response):
cachekey = request.headers.get('X-Cache-Key')
if(request.method=="GET"):
cache.set(cachekey,str(response.data).encode("utf8"))
return response

class AppdateTime :
def __init__(self, day, date, time):
self.day = day
self.date = date
self.time = time
```

```
@app.route("/")
def hello():

    # Rest Python implementation removed for brevity
```

The aforementioned Python code does the following:

- Line 4 imports the `memcache` module

- Next, we make the connection to the `memcached` server running on `127.0.0.1:11211`

- The `processResponse` method marked with `@app.after_request` executes for every request

- The `processResponse` method adds the response to the memcached server against the key specified in the request header (`X-Cache-key`)

# Measuring gains

It is time to test the changes and make sure that they have given any performance gain. It is important to note that we cannot apply the baselines developed in the previous chapter as the complete setup is quite different. We are no longer serving static content; here we are building dynamic content from a proxy server. Thus, first we need to perform a couple of tests in order to build a baseline with only the proxy server:

```
$ siege -b -c 250 -r 50 -q http://192.168.2.100/python/
done.
Transactions: 12461 hits
Availability: 99.69 %
Data transferred: 6.03 MB
Response time: 0.33 secs
Transaction rate: 381.65 trans/sec
Throughput: 0.18 MB/sec
Concurrency: 127.28
Successful transactions: 12461
Failed transactions: 39
```

Now, modify the NGINX configuration to serve content using the memcached server. Validated by the new numbers, the server will take much more load. Increase the concurrency so that you can get to know the new limits:

```
$ siege -b -c 900 -r 50 -q http://192.168.2.100/python/
done.
```

```
Transactions: 45000 hits
Availability: 100.00 %
Elapsed time: 18.15 secs
Data transferred: 23.82 MB
Response time: 0.27 secs
Transaction rate: 2479.34 trans/sec
Throughput: 1.31 MB/sec
Concurrency: 669.05
Successful transactions: 45000
Failed transactions: 0
```

# Summary

This chapter is aimed to explain the caching capabilities of NGINX. It is capable of caching all static and dynamic content. The open_file_cache directive can be used to improve NGINX performance while serving static content.

The dynamic content caching has a couple of options. NGINX can interface with other servers/applications using different protocols, such as FastCGI, HTTP Proxy, uwsgi, and so on. Depending upon the type of interface, the related cache can be employed. This chapter gave examples of PHP and Python in order to show how NGINX can work with other servers while utilizing the corresponding caches. NGINX can also be used to serve content from the memcached server. The last part of the chapter demonstrated NGINX's ability to work with memcache.

It is important to note that caching will improve performance, but not all data can be cached. Any data that is highly time sensitive or varies with the content of the request should not be cached. The impact of caching must also be measured by doing performance tests. The results should be used to alter the application baselines.

NGINX is completely extensible; thus, it allows us to write custom extensions to do varied things. The large catalog of NGINX extensions is a statement of its easy extensibility. In the next chapter, we will talk about how to extend NGINX and build performance-oriented plugins using Lua.

# Extending NGINX

Until now, we have installed and configured NGINX for out-of-the-box request processing. However, NGINX is completely extensible, which essentially means that if we are not satisfied with what it does, we can build custom scripts to enable the same. The Lua scripting language can be used to leverage NGINX's extension hooks for custom request processing.

In this chapter, we will cover the following topics:

- The Lua scripting language
- The NGINX Lua module
- The NGINX Lua API
- Setting up the server

## The Lua scripting language

Lua is a lightweight, multi-paradigm programming language built on top of ANSI C. It is a dynamically typed language, which is intended for scripting purposes. It can be used on platforms ranging from large server systems to small mobile applications. The Lua interpreter is quite compact and can be embedded in various applications.

Lua is a functional language and provides a small set of general features, such as functions, garbage collection, closures, coercion, coroutine, and so on. It only supports a limited set of data structures, such as Boolean, numbers, strings, and tables (for arrays, sets, lists, and so on). All code in Lua is written as blocks of statements, optionally followed by a semicolon.

The Lua code can be executed with LuaJIT, a just-in-time compiler for Lua. The interpreter can be used in the interactive mode, so let's try a few simple examples to get hands-on with Lua. This section only provides a brief overview of Lua's syntax and features. For a complete overview, refer to the official documentation.

Let's start by downloading the latest version of LuaJIT from `http://luajit.org/ download.html`:

```
$ wget http://luajit.org/download/LuaJIT-2.0.3.tar.gz
$ tar -xvzf LuaJIT-2.0.3.tar.gz


$ ls LuaJIT-2.0.3


COPYRIGHT doc dynasm etc Makefile README src
```

In order to build LuaJIT, we need to invoke the `make` command:

```
$ make
==== Building LuaJIT 2.0.3 ====
make -C src
….．．．．
==== Successfully built LuaJIT 2.0.3 ====
```

The generated LuaJIT binary can be installed using the `install` option of the `make` command:

```
$ sudo make install
==== Installing LuaJIT 2.0.3 to /usr/local ====
….．．．．．
ln -sf luajit-2.0.3 /usr/local/bin/luajit
==== Successfully installed LuaJIT 2.0.3 to /usr/local ====
```

Now that we have installed the Lua interpreter, execute the `luajit` command with the `-v` option to check the version information:

```
$ luajit -v
LuaJIT 2.0.3 -- Copyright (C) 2005-2015 Mike Pall. http://luajit.org/
```

Let's try our first sample to build the `hello` function. The function takes a name and then prints a greeting message:

```
    $ luajit
    LuaJIT 2.0.3 -- Copyright (C) 2005-2015 Mike Pall. http://luajit.org/
    > function hello(name)
    >> print ("hello "..name)
    >> print ("let's run Lua")
    >> end
```

```
> hello("rahul")
hello rahul
let's run Lua
```

There are a couple of things to note:

- The first statement defines a function with the name argument.
- The method starts from the function statement until it finds the end statement.
- Messages can be sent to the console using the print API.
- In the second line, string concatenation has been performed using the . . . operator.

The previous example demonstrated Lua functions and the string data type. In the next example, we compute the factorial of a number to demonstrate a few more features, such as loops, variables, return values, and so on:

```
$ luajit
LuaJIT 2.0.3 -- Copyright (C) 2005-2015 Mike Pall. http://luajit.org/
> function computeFactorial(num)
>> local fact = 1
>> for i = 2,num do
>> fact=fact*i
>> end
>> return fact
>> end
> start = 5
>> while start < 10 do
>> print(start,computeFactorial(start))
>> start = start+1
>> end
5       120
6       720
7       5040
8       40320
9       362880
>
```

In the preceding code, we built the `computeFactorial` function. The function takes a number and returns its factorial. There are a couple of things to note:

- The second line demonstrates variable scopes as it creates the `fact` variable available only in the `computeFactorial` method
- The third line defines a `for` loop iterating from 2 to the passed value
- The `for` loop defined in the third line ends with the `end` statement in the fifth line
- The function returns the value and ends with the `end` statement (the seventh line)
- The code finds a `while` loop (in the ninth line) to compute the factorials of a few numbers
- The print API prints the factorials as key-value pairs (in the tenth line)

Now that we have gained some knowledge of Lua, we want to explore the NGINX-Lua integration for custom request processing.

# The NGINX Lua module

NGINX has the `nginx_lua` module developed by **Openresty.org** that can be used to leverage Lua scripting. The module integrates Lua threads into the NGINX event model to enable asynchronous code execution. The module shares the loaded Lua libraries across all requests but segregates request contexts using Lua threads, thus resulting in a small memory footprint.

Openresty.org provides a complete web server package with an NGINX core, `nginx_lua`, LuaJIT, and a host of NGINX modules that can be used to deploy applications.

# Installation

This module is not enabled by default and needs to be built with NGINX. The module requires the Lua 5.1 version with the LuaJIT 2.0/ 2.1 interpreter. Download the latest version of the module from `https://github.com/openresty/lua-nginx-module/releases`. You can also use the following command:

```
$ wget https://github.com/openresty/lua-nginx-
module/archive/v0.9.15.tar.gz

$ tar -xzvf v0.9.15.tar.gz
```

The module also requires `ngx_develt_kit`. The latest version of the kit can be downloaded from `https://github.com/simpl/ngx_devel_kit/releases`. You can also use the following command:

```
$ wget https://github.com/simpl/ngx_devel_kit/archive/v0.2.19.tar.gz
$ tar -xzvf v0.2.19.tar.gz
```

We need to build these modules with NGINX, but before we do that, we need to export Lua and the LuaJIT library as system variables. Lua and LuaJIT should be available in `/usr/local/lib/lua/` and `/usr/local/include/luajit-2.0` respectively:

```
$ export LUAJIT_LIB=/usr/local/lib
$ export LUAJIT_INC=/usr/local/include/luajit-2.0
```

Next, configure NGINX to build the downloaded modules using the `configure` command. In addition to configuring the modules using the `--add-module` option, we also need to specify the `luajit` binary path to the linker:

```
$ ./configure \
 --with-ld-opt='-Wl,-Bsymbolic-functions -Wl,-z,relro,-rpath,/usr/local/bin/luajit' \
 --prefix=/usr/share/nginx –conf-path=/etc/nginx/nginx.conf \
 --http-log-path=/var/log/nginx/access.log \
 --error-log-path=/var/log/nginx/error.log \
 --lock-path=/var/lock/nginx.lock \
 --pid-path=/run/nginx.pid \
 --http-client-body-temp-path=/var/lib/nginx/body \
 --http-fastcgi-temp-path=/var/lib/nginx/fastcgi \
 --http-proxy-temp-path=/var/lib/nginx/proxy \
 --http-scgi-temp-path=/var/lib/nginx/scgi \
 --http-uwsgi-temp-path=/var/lib/nginx/uwsgi \
 --with-pcre-jit \
 --with-http_realip_module \
 --with-http_addition_module \
 --with-http_sub_module \
 --with-pcre=/home/ubuntu/nginx/pcre-8.36 \
 --add-module=/home/ubuntu/nginx/ngx_devel_kit-0.2.19 \
 --add-module=/home/ubuntu/nginx/lua-nginx-module-0.9.15
```

After configuring the NGINX build, generate, and install the binary using `make` commands, as shown here:

```
$ make
$ sudo make install
```

Validate the NGINX installation using the `-V` option:

```
$ nginx -V
nginx version: nginx/1.7.9
built by gcc 4.8.2 (Ubuntu 4.8.2-19ubuntu1)
configure arguments: -with-ld-opt='-Wl,-Bsymbolic-functions -Wl,
-z,relro,-rpath,/usr/local/bin/luajit' --prefix=/usr/share/nginx
--conf-path=/etc/nginx/nginx.conf --http-log-
path=/var/log/nginx/access.log --error-log-
path=/var/log/nginx/error.log --lock-path=/var/lock/nginx.lock --pid-
path=/run/nginx.pid --http-client-body-temp-path=/var/lib/nginx/body
--http-fastcgi-temp-path=/var/lib/nginx/fastcgi --http-proxy-temp-
path=/var/lib/nginx/proxy --http-scgi-temp-path=/var/lib/nginx/scgi -
-http-uwsgi-temp-path=/var/lib/nginx/uwsgi --with-pcre-jit --with-
http_realip_module --with-http_addition_module --with-http_sub_module
--with-pcre=/home/ubuntu/nginx/pcre-8.36 --add-
module=/home/ubuntu/nginx/ngx_devel_kit-0.2.19 --add-
module=/home/ubuntu/nginx/lua-nginx-module-0.9.15
```

> On some platforms, the `nginx -V` command may give the following error due to the loading of shared libraries:
>
> ```
> error while loading shared libraries: libluajit-
> 5.1.so.2: cannot open shared object file: No such file
> or directory
> ```
>
> In order to fix the error, append the `/usr/local/lib/` path to the shared library path by executing the following command:
>
> ```
> $ LD_LIBRARY_PATH=/usr/local/lib/:$LD_LIBRARY_PATH
> ```

# Directives

While working with Lua directives, it is important to understand that NGINX processes a request in different life cycle phases. Each of the NGINX modules is executed in one of these phases. The following is a list of important phases of the NGINX request life cycle:

- **Location selection phase**: The server selects the location block to serve the request

- **Location rewrite phase**: `HttpRewriteModule` is executed in this phase if the request requires a location rewrite
- **Access phase**: `HttpAccessModule` is executed in this phase to determine whether the request should be allowed, denied, or authenticated
- **Try files phase**: The request tries to get a response using the `try_files` block
- **Content phase**: A response is generated in this phase using one of the various content handlers in NGINX, for example, Proxy, FastCGI, and so on
- **Log phase**: An access log is generated in this phase for the served request

The `ngx_lua` module provides the following directives to enable execution of the Lua code in one of the phases of NGINX execution.

# lua_package_path

This directive specifies the lookup path for Lua scripts used in `set_by_lua`, `content_by_lua`, and other directives.

# lua_shared_dict

This directive creates a Lua dictionary that is shared across all NGINX workers.

# init_by_lua/init_by_lua_file

This directive specifies the Lua code (as a string) executed by NGINX's master process at the global Lua VM level. The code can register Lua's global variables and import Lua modules that can be used later in other Lua directives. Here's an example:

```
init_by_lua 'cjson = require "cjson"';
```

The `init_by_lua_file` directive is similar to `init_by_lua`. It executes the code specified in a file to set the global context. Both directives are available under the `http` section of an NGINX configuration.

# set_by_lua/set_by_lua_file

This directive specifies the Lua code (as a string), a `return` variable, and certain optional arguments. It executes the code using the passed arguments and provides the value in the specified variable. Here's an example:

```
set_by_lua $sum 'return (10 + 20)';
echo $sum;
```

Arguments passed to the Lua code can be accessed using the ngx.arg[i] directive. The directive can only return a single value from the code. If multiple values are required, we need to use the ngx.var.VariableName directive to create multiple variables. Here's an example:

```
set_by_lua $sum 'return (ngx.arg[1] + ngx.arg[2])' 10 20;
echo $sum;
```

The set_by_lua_file directive is similar to set_by_lua. It executes the code specified in a file using optional parameters and returns the value in the specified variable. Both directives are available under the if (in location), location, and server sections of an NGINX configuration.

## content_by_lua/content_by_lua_file

This directive acts as a content provider and executes the Lua code (as a string) to generate an NGINX response. It is important to note that the directive must not be used with other content handles, such as Proxy, in the same location block.

The content_by_lua_file directive is similar to content_by_lua. It executes the code specified in a file to generate an NGINX response. Both directives are available under the location and if (in location) sections of an NGINX configuration. Here's an example:

```
location /content {
    content_by_lua 'ngx.say("hello ! Content from lua")';
}
```

## header_filter_by_lua/header_filter_by_lua_file

NGINX allows the manipulation of response headers using Lua. The code can add new header fields or manipulate/delete existing response headers. The header_filter_by_lua directive executes the Lua code as a response header filter. The code can access response headers using ngx.header.HeaderFieldName variable.

The header_filter_by_lua_file directive is similar to header_filter_by_lua. It executes the code specified in a file to manipulate response headers. Both directives are available under the http, server, location, and if (in location) sections of an NGINX configuration. Here's an example:

```
location /content {
    content_by_lua 'ngx.say("hello ! Content from lua")';
    header_filter_by_lua 'ngx.header.X-Source = "LuaScript"';
}
```

# body_filter_by_lua/body_filter_by_lua_file

The directive executes during the `output-body-filter` phase of NGINX and can be used to manipulate the output body. The complete response body is passed in the `ngx.arg[1]` variable. The Lua code can alter the contents of the variable to return a new output body. The `ngx.arg[2]` variable contains the `eof` flag.

The `body_filter_by_lua_file` directive is similar to `body_filter_by_lua`. It executes the code specified in a file to filter the output body. Both directives are available under the `http`, `server`, `location`, and `if` (in `location`) sections of an NGINX configuration. Here's an example:

```
location /content {
    content_by_lua 'ngx.say("hello ! Content from lua")';
    header_filter_by_lua 'ngx.header.content_length = nil';
    body_filter_by_lua '
      ngx.arg[1]=string.upper("from body filer"..ngx.arg[1]) ';
}
```

> In the HTTP protocol, the `Content-Length` header field signifies the length of the message body. On the client side, the protocol determines the size of the message transferred, known as the transfer length. The two lengths should be the same. If the two lengths are going to be different, then the length of the message body should not be specified. Thus, it is always recommended that you clear the `Content-Length` header field when the Lua code modifies the body length.

# access_by_lua/access_by_lua_file

The directive executes the Lua code during the access phase of NGINX after the execution of `ngx_http_access_module`.

The `access_by_lua_file` directive is similar to `access_by_lua`. It executes code specified in a file to determine access. Both directives are available under the `http`, `server`, `location`, and `if` (in `location`) sections of an NGINX configuration. Here's an example:

```
location /content {
    content_by_lua 'ngx.say("hello ! Content from lua")';
    access_by_lua ' if ngx.var.remote_addr == "192.168.2.111" then
          ngx.exit(ngx.HTTP_FORBIDDEN)
        end';
}
```

## rewrite_by_lua/rewrite_by_lua_file

The `rewrite_by_lua` directive executes Lua code during the rewrite phase of NGINX after the execution of `ngx_http_rewrite_module`.

The `rewrite_by_lua_file` directive is similar to `rewrite_by_lua`. It executes the code specified in a file during the rewrite phase. Both directives are available under the `http`, `server`, `location`, and `if (in location)` sections of an NGINX configuration. Here's an example:

```
location /content {
    content_by_lua 'ngx.say("hello ! Content from lua")';
    rewrite_by_lua ' if ngx.var.remote_addr == "192.168.2.111" then
            ngx.redirect("/forbidden.html")
        end';
}
```

## log_by_lua/log_by_lua_file

The `log_by_lua` directive executes the Lua code during the `log` request phase of NGINX. The code does not replace NGINX access logs, but can do sundry things, such as tracking request times, logging messages, and so on. The messages logged using `ngx.log()` will be sent to the NGINX error log. It is important to note that the request body is not accessible in this API.

The `log_by_lua_file` directive is similar to `log_by_lua`. It executes the code specified in a file during the `log-request` phase. Both directives are available under the `http`, `server`, `location`, and `if (in location)` sections of an NGINX configuration. Here's an example:

```
location /content {
    echo "hello world!"
    log_by_lua 'ngx.log(ngx.NOTICE,"logging request response")';
}
```

# The NGINX-Lua API

The `nginx_lua` module provides an API that can be called in the Lua code to interact with other NGINX components. The complete API is exposed in the form of two packages, namely, `ngx` and `ndk`. These packages are available within the `ngx_lua` directive and can be imported in external Lua modules using the `require` statements. The API has been integrated into the NGINX event loop, so all I/O operations in the Lua code must be performed using the exposed API to avoid performance bottlenecks.

The complete API is quite comprehensive and provides methods to interact with every feature of NGINX. It is available at `http://wiki.nginx.org/HttpLuaModule#Nginx_API_for_Lua`. The following section provides an overview of the exposed API.

# ngx.arg

The `ngx.arg[i]` API provides a way to access the variable/data passed to the Lua code:

- In the `set_by_lua` directive, the variable holds the passed arguments
- In the `body_filter_by_lua` directive, the variable holds the response body and the `eof` flag

# ngx.var.varName

Any variable declared in an NGINX configuration can be accessed using the `ngx.var.varName` variable. The Lua code can read and write values in these variables. No new variables can be declared by Lua using this syntax.

# ngx.say/ngx.print

The function writes output from the Lua code to the response body.

# ngx.location.capture/ngx.location.capture_multi

The `ngx.location.capture` API is a function call that can be used to send a subrequest. The method takes the URI as the argument and returns a response containing the response header, response body, and response status. Optionally, we can also specify additional parameters, such as the HTTP method, arguments, and so on, in the function call.

The `ngx.location.capture_multi` API is similar to the `ngx.location.capture` API, but it can issue multiple, parallel subrequests to multiple URIs. The function takes input arguments as an array of URIs and option pairs. It returns multiple values—one for each URI passed. Here's an example:

```
res= ngx.location.capture('/call')

res1, res2, res3 = ngx.location.capture_multi{
    { "/call1", { args = "v1=1&v2=3" } },
```

```
    { "/call2" },
    { "/call3", { method = ngx.HTTP_POST, body = "Data" } }, }
```

# ngx.ctx

This API can be used to hold data specific to the current request.

# ngx.status

This API denotes the response status of the current request.

# ngx.header.HeaderField

This API can be used to access/manipulate response headers. Besides modifying the existing headers, the Lua code can also define new header fields. Setting the value to `nil` clears the `header` field.

# ngx.req.functions

This API defines a number of methods in the `ngx.req` package that can be used to manipulate the current request. The following is a list of the available methods:

- `start_time`: This returns the timestamp of when the request was created.

- `http_version`: This returns the HTTP version of the current request.

- `raw_header`: This returns the HTTP header of the current request.

- `get_method`/`set_method`: This retrieves/manipulates the current request's HTTP method.

- `get_headers`/`set_header`/`clear_header`: This retrieves/manipulates the current request's HTTP headers. Modifying or adding (new) a header field is allowed by the API. The header field can be removed by either setting the value to `nil` or by using the `clear_header` function.

- `read_body`/`discard_body`: This API reads the current request body if it has not been read previously. If the body has been read earlier, the method returns immediately. Alternatively, the Lua code can discard a request by issuing the `discard_body` call.

- `get_body_data`/`set_body_data`/`get_post_args`: These methods allow the Lua code to read and manipulate the response body as a string. If the request is a HTTP post request, then use the `get_post_args` function call to get data as variables instead of strings.

- `set_uri`: This call can modify the URI of the current request. The method can also trigger new location matching in NGINX, such as the rewrite directive. By default, the location jumping is turned off.

- `set_uri_args`/`get_uri_args`: These methods can use the read and modify request query string. The `get` method returns the complete parameters as key-value pairs.

# ngx.shared.DictionaryName

This API can be used to access a shared dictionary created by the `lua_shared_dict` directive. The dictionary has the following methods:

- `get`/`get_stale`: This method returns the value for the key passed. If the key does not exist, the method returns `null`. If the key has expired, the `get_stale` method returns the expired value.

- `set`/`safe_set`: This method sets key-value pairs. Optionally, the method can also specify the expiry time during which the value would be valid. The `set` method would always override the value of the key even if it has not expired. Alternatively, the `safe_set` method will never override a nonexpired value.

- `flush_all`/`flush_expired`: The `flush_all` method marks all the items in the dictionary as expired. The `flush_expired` method frees up memory by removing all the expired items.

- `delete`: This removes a key-value pair from the dictionary.

- `get_keys`: This returns all keys to the dictionary.

# ngx.socket.tcp

This API can be used to work with a `tcp` or `unix` socket. The API is completely nonblocking in nature. It is important to note that the socket has the lifetime of the Lua code executing it. Thus, it cannot be shared across various Lua handlers.

The socket created by the API offers the following methods:

- `connect`: This method connects to a `tcp` socket address or a `unix` socket address.

- `sslhandshake`: This attempts an SSL handshake over the connection.

- `send`: This writes data over the wire.

- `receive`/`receiveuntil`: This receives data over the wire. The `receiveuntil` method returns an iterator that can be used to read a stream.

- `close`: This closes the connection.

- `settimeout`: This method sets a timeout for the next operation over the socket, namely connect, send, read, and so on.

- `setkeepalive`: This adds the connection to Lua's internal connection pool. The pool has a fixed size, specified as an argument in `setkeepalive`. If the pool exceeds the size, then the least recently used connection is automatically closed. The pool also specifies a lifetime for the connection, after which the connection is closed.

The socket is automatically closed when the Lua code exits or the socket lifetime expires. Any fatal error occurring over the socket will close the socket.

# NGINX Lua libraries

The NGINX-Lua support is quite mature. Besides the module and the API, there are a couple of third-party libraries that can be used for various purposes. The following is a list of a few of the available libraries:

- `lua-resty-mysql` (`github.com/openresty/lua-resty-mysql`): This library provides the `Mysql` driver to Lua

- `lus-resty-redis` (`github.com/openresty/lua-resty-redis`): This library provides the Redis driver to Lua

- `lua-resty-memcached` (`github.com/openresty/lua-resty-memcached`): This library provides the memcached driver to Lua

- `lua-resty-string` (`github.com/openresty/lua-resty-string`): This library provides string utility methods

- `lua-resty-websocket` (`github.com/openresty/lua-resty-websocket`): This library provides support for WebSockets in Lua

- `lua-resty-dns` (`github.com/openresty/lua-resty-dns`): This library provides the DNS resolver in Lua

- `lua-resty-upload` (`github.com/openresty/lua-resty-upload`): This library provides support for the upload of HTTP files in Lua

In order to use these libraries, include the respective scripts in the NGINX configuration file using the `lua_package_path` directive. Then, import the package using Lua's `require` statement:

```
lua_package_path "/home/ubuntu/lua-resty-mysql-master/lib/?.lua;;";
init_by_lua 'mysql = require "resty.mysql"';
```

# Setting up the server

In the following section, we will try to build an example using NGINX-Lua support.

## The problem statement

Let's say we have a website, the pages of which have moved from location `/previous-feature/1` , ... , `/previous-feature/n` to `/new-feature-1` , ... , `/new-feature-n`. Now, if the site is being indexed by Google (or any other search engine), it might be required to perform URL redirects when the Googlebot hits `/previous-location/X`. The redirect may require a proper HTTP redirect code (`301`, `302`) too.

## Statement

In order to solve the previously stated problem, we need to do some validation before processing a request. We will configure NGINX to do the following:

* Determine whether the request URI is one of the redirected locations
* If no, then serve the request
* If yes, then determine the new location and HTTP redirect code
* Perform an NGINX redirect to the new location using the redirect code

We will save the location information in MySQL in the following format; then, we can do lookups from NGINX to determine whether the location requires a redirect or not:

| ID | Org_Location | Redirect_Loc | Redirect_Code |
|----|--------------|--------------|---------------|
| 1 | /previous-feature/1 | /new-feature-1 | 301 |
| 2 | /previous-feature/2 | /new-feature-2 | 302 |

The following MySQL statements will create the required table and insert data into it:

```
CREATE TABLE seo_redirect_location (
 id int(11) NOT NULL AUTO_INCREMENT,
 Org_Location varchar(45) DEFAULT NULL,
 Redirect_Location varchar(45) DEFAULT NULL,
 Redirect_Code int(11) NOT NULL,
 PRIMARY KEY (id)
);

INSERT INTO seo_redirect_location
(Org_Location, Redirect_Location, Redirect_Code)
```

```
VALUES
('/previous-feature/1','/new-feature-1',301);

INSERT INTO seo_redirect_location
(Org_Location,Redirect_Location, Redirect_Code)
VALUES
('/previous-feature/2','/new-feature-2',302);
```

Now, we need to build the NGINX script that can look up the MySQL database. We will add the `lua-resty-Mysql` library to do this. The following NGINX script sums up all the required changes:

```
# add library to path
lua_package_path "/home/ubuntu/lua-resty-mysql-
master/lib/?.lua;;";

# import mysql package
init_by_lua 'mysql = require "resty.mysql" ';

server {
 location / {
      default_type 'text/plain';

      content_by_lua ' local db, err = mysql:new()
        db:set_timeout(1000)
#connect to databas
        local ok, err, errno, sqlstate = db:connect{
            host = "192.168.2.111",
            port = 3306,
            database = "test",
            user = "newuser",
            password = "newuser",
            max_packet_size = 1024 * 1024 }

        if not ok then
          ngx.exec("@inline_concat")
        end

        local res, err, errno, sqlstate = db:query("select * from
seo_redirect_location where org_Location=\'"..ngx.var.uri.."\'
order by id asc", 10)

        if next(res) then
          return ngx.redirect(res[1].Redirect_location,res[1].
Redirect_Code)
```

```
        end
        ngx.exec("@inline_concat")
        ';
    }

    location @inline_concat {
      # MIME type determined by default_type:
      default_type 'text/plain';
      set $a "hello";
      set $b "world";
      # Lua script to generate Hello world
        set_by_lua $res "return
ngx.arg[1]..ngx.arg[2]..ngx.var.uri" $a $b;

        return 200 $res;
    }
}
```

The preceding script does the following things:

- The `lua_package_path` directive adds the `lua-resty-Mysql` scripts to the NGINX Lua path

- The `init_by_lua` directive imports the `resty.mysql` package

- NGINX does all validations in the default location block

- The `content_by_lua` directive tries to build a response using Lua

- The `db.connect` statement connects to the MySQL instance

- If an error occurs while connecting to MySQL, then the content is served from the `@inline_concat` location

- If no error occurs, then check the location int in the `seo_redirect_location` table using `db:query()` method

- The `next()` method call gives back any result found by the query

- If one exists, perform a redirect using the `ngx.redirect()` method

- If one does not exist, the server serves content from the `@inline_concat` location

- If the NGINX configuration does not have a default content type, it needs to be set in the `@inline_concat` location block

- In the `@inline_concat` location, `set_by_lua` executes the Lua code to generate a response

- NGINX sends back the generated response using the `return` statement. The optional HTTP code (200) is also passed to the call

# Summary

The chapter is aimed at extending NGINX request processing using Lua. Lua is a powerful, dynamic scripting language. This language implements a small set of features. It has a rather small memory footprint and can be embedded on various host systems using the LuaJIT interpreter. NGINX has the `ngx_lua` module, which enables Lua scripts in NGINX request processing. This chapter described the module directives and their integration into the life cycle phases of NGINX requests.

The NGINX-Lua integration also provides an API, exposed as the `ngx` and `ndk` packages. These packages can be used to interact with other NGINX components. The packages can also be imported into external Lua scripts. The API has been integrated with the NGINX event loop. Thus, all I/O should be performed using these packages to avoid a performance hit. In the end, the chapter used the module directives, API, and third-party Lua libraries to build an example of custom request processing.

# Index

## A

**Apache JMeter**
**Apache JMeter, components**

## B

## C

## D

**directives**
**dynamic content, caching**

## Thank you for buying
# NGINX High Performance

## About Packt Publishing

Packt, pronounced 'packed', published its first book, *Mastering phpMyAdmin for Effective MySQL Management*, in April 2004, and subsequently continued to specialize in publishing highly focused books on specific technologies and solutions.

Our books and publications share the experiences of your fellow IT professionals in adapting and customizing today's systems, applications, and frameworks. Our solution-based books give you the knowledge and power to customize the software and technologies you're using to get the job done. Packt books are more specific and less general than the IT books you have seen in the past. Our unique business model allows us to bring you more focused information, giving you more of what you need to know, and less of what you don't.

Packt is a modern yet unique publishing company that focuses on producing quality, cutting-edge books for communities of developers, administrators, and newbies alike. For more information, please visit our website at www.packtpub.com.

## About Packt Open Source

In 2010, Packt launched two new brands, Packt Open Source and Packt Enterprise, in order to continue its focus on specialization. This book is part of the Packt Open Source brand, home to books published on software built around open source licenses, and offering information to anybody from advanced developers to budding web designers. The Open Source brand also runs Packt's Open Source Royalty Scheme, by which Packt gives a royalty to each open source project about whose software a book is sold.

## Writing for Packt

We welcome all inquiries from people who are interested in authoring. Book proposals should be sent to author@packtpub.com. If your book idea is still at an early stage and you would like to discuss it first before writing a formal book proposal, then please contact us; one of our commissioning editors will get in touch with you.

We're not just looking for published authors; if you have strong technical skills but no writing experience, our experienced editors can help you develop a writing career, or simply get some additional reward for your expertise.

## Nginx HTTP Server
## Second Edition

ISBN: 978-1-78216-232-2          Paperback: 318 pages

Make the most of your infrastructure and serve pages faster than ever with Nginx

1. Complete configuration directive and module reference.

2. Discover possible interactions between Nginx and Apache to get the best of both worlds.

3. Learn to configure your servers and virtual hosts efficiently.

4. A step-by-step guide to switching from Apache to Nginx.

## Mastering NGINX

ISBN: 978-1-84951-744-7          Paperback: 322 pages

An in-depth guide to configuring NGINX for any situation, including numerous examples and reference tables describing each directive

1. An in-depth configuration guide to help you understand how to best configure NGINX for any situation.

2. Includes useful code samples to help you integrate NGINX into your application architecture.

3. Full of example configuration snippets, best-practice descriptions, and reference tables for each directive.

Please check **www.PacktPub.com** for information on our titles

## Nginx Module Extension

ISBN: 978-1-78216-304-6    Paperback: 128 pages

Customize and regulate the robust Nginx web server, and write your own Nginx modules efficiently

1. Install Nginx from its source on multiple platforms.

2. Become acquainted with core Nginx modules and their configuration options.

3. Explore optional and third-party module extensions along with configuration directives.

## Instant Nginx Starter

ISBN: 978-1-78216-512-5    Paperback: 48 pages

Implement the nifty features of nginx with this focused guide

1. Learn something new in an Instant! A short, fast, focused guide delivering immediate results.

2. Understand Nginx and its relevance to the modern Web.

3. Install Nginx and explore the different methods of installation.

4. Configure and customize Nginx.

Please check **www.PacktPub.com** for information on our titles

9 781785 281839